The Care of the Earth

FACETS

Selected Titles in the Facets Series

The Care of the Earth

Joseph Sittler

Introduction by
Martin E. Marty

Fortress Press
Minneapolis

THE CARE OF THE EARTH

Fortress Press Facets edition 2004

Adapted from *The Care of the Earth and Other University Sermons,*
© 1964 Fortress Press.

Scriptural translations are quoted or adapted from the Revised Standard Version of the Bible, copyright © 1946, 1952, 1971 by the Division of Christian Education of the National Council of the Churches of Christ in the USA. Used by permission.

Cover design: James Korsmo
Cover image: Myanmar (Burma)/Mouths of the Irrawaddy. NASA Johnson Space Center–Earth Sciences and Image Analysis (NASA-JSC-ES&IA). Used by Permission.
Book design: Joseph Bonyata

Library of Congress Cataloging-in-Publication Data

Sittler, Joseph.
  The care of the earth / Joseph Sittler ; with an introduction by Martin E. Marty.–[Rev. ed.].
      p. cm. — (Facets)
   Includes bibliographical references.
   ISBN 0-8006-3688-0 (alk. paper)
   1. Universities and colleges–Sermons. 2. Sermons, American–20th century. I. Title. II. Facets (Fortress Press)
   BV4310.S47 2004
   252'.041–dc22

                                              2004020226

The paper used in this publication meets the minimum requirements of American National Standard for Information Sciences — Permanence of Paper for Printed Library Materials, ANSI Z329.48-1984.

Manufactured in the U.S.A.

08   07   06   05   04   1   2   3   4   5   6   7   8   9   10

Contents

Introduction
by Martin E. Marty

"Discovery is our business." So, in translation, reads a framed calligraphic Chinese motto that faces me every day.

Once it graced the wall of Nobelist Charles Huggins, but could easily have been the banner of theologian Joseph Sittler.

Professor Sittler was the most sense-ripened person I have known; and he used his senses, even when they were dimmed and dulled, to discover. Touch: when blind, he rubbed his callused finger over his profile in bronze on the Joseph Sittler medal and when he came to the largish nose pronounced, "They've got it right!" Smell: he would discover new levels of mysticism when he would attend the Divine Liturgy at the Russian Orthodox Cathedral: God was discernible in the mists of incense. Sight: "If you were given vision back for an hour, what would you look at?" Sittler: "The blue glass at Chartres Cathedral." Sound? "Faith comes by hearing," as he makes clear in this book, attentive as he is in it to the sacrament of sound waves and the task of listening with care. Again: "What would you say to someone who would reform the church today?" Sittler: "I'd say, 'Watch your language,'" as he did.

Discovery was always Sittler's business. Many think that the Chinese motto applies only to the Hugginses of the world, the scientific discoverers. But for Sittler, divine discovery occurred in the muck of the human record. He would see the sacred teased out of texts—note what he unearths in the so-familiar biblical passages that follow. Or he would seek to discover as he showed awareness of acts of mercy and love. One could pass a phenomenon a thousand times and then, with Sittler as a guide, could suddenly discover what it had been about all along. Note for yourself as you read.

Calling this collection *The Care of the Earth* may sound like false advertising, since this is not a conventional environmental text. It is much more than that. The key word is "care." Sittler helps us discover new ways to care in responding to nature, to human signals, to beauty, to the promptings of the heart, to the Word of God. Care for the kingdom, and all "these things" such as improved natural environment "will be added." Here, as often, grace and nature intersect, overlap, and interfuse each other. Sittler would call that gospel.

The Care of the Earth

1
How to Read a Parable

He said also to the man who had invited him, "When you give a dinner or a banquet, do not invite your friends or your brothers or your kinsmen or rich neighbors, lest they also invite you in return, and you be repaid. But when you give a feast, invite the poor, the maimed, the lame, the blind, and you will be blessed, because they cannot repay you. You will be repaid at the resurrection of the just."

When one of those who sat at table with him heard this, he said to him, "Blessed is he who shall eat bread in the kingdom of God!" But he said to him, "A man once gave a great banquet, and invited many; and at the time for the banquet he sent his servant to say to those who had been invited, 'Come; for all is now ready.' But they all alike began to make excuses. The first said to him, 'I have bought a field, and I must go out and see it; I pray you, have me excused.' And another said, 'I

*have bought five yoke of oxen, and I go to
examine them; I pray you, have me excused.'
And another said, 'I have married a wife, and
therefore I cannot come.' So the servant came
and reported this to his master. Then the
householder in anger said to his servant, 'Go
out quickly to the streets and lanes of the city,
and bring in the poor and maimed and blind
and lame.' And the servant said, 'Sir, what
you commanded has been done, and still there
is room.' And the master said to the servant,
'Go out to the highways and hedges, and compel people to come in, that my house may be
filled. For I tell you, none of those men who
were invited shall taste my banquet.'"*

—Luke 14:12-24

Jesus spoke about hearing in several ways.
He certainly admonished people that they
hear, to be careful of what they hear, and
even more careful about how they interpret
and understand what they hear. How one
hears was apparently as important for him as
what one hears.

As we consider this parable concerning
the man who gave a dinner and invited
many, our intention is to take care how we
hear. And if we learn how to listen to this
parable we shall gain a double benefit; we
shall hear a word of God that has unusual
and disturbing meaning for our time and cir-

cumstances, and we shall gain competence for hearing all the parables. If we do not hear properly we shall certainly neither understand correctly nor respond justly.

Different kinds of speech require different levels of hearing. One does not listen to directions for opening a can of paint at the same level as is necessary when one listens to a poem, or play, or an examination question. As we listen to the parables of Jesus we must know at the outset that these packed stories are not little parcels of the obvious, or extended epigrams that enclose folk-wisdom, or simply sly observations by a discerning raconteur of the spiritual life. They are, quite bluntly, *words of life*—for they are the passionate words into which Jesus poured the concentrated meaning of human existence before God.

Two requirements, then, as we listen. We must, first, put our listening ears into the situation into which the parable was spoken. That would seem to be easy, but I would remind you that a considerable part of literary and historical study in a university bears evidence that it is hard.

Suppose, for an instance, that we had no records of Abraham Lincoln's pre-presidential life but records only of his deeds and words following his election to the Presidency. And suppose, further, that Mr. Lincoln had not written a word—so that all we knew of him came from later reports of friends, fellow party members, people passionately devoted to his memory and purposes. The purposes and plans of such reporters moreover, were wrought out on a vast international scene far removed from New Salem, Springfield, and the Illinois prairie. All the anecdotes, speeches, epigrams of Lincoln would, in such a case, come to us in a context not completely discontinuous with but surely other and more complicated than the context of the reported actions and utterances.

The duty of the historian in such a situation is to disengage the actions and utterances from the changes and expanded context. The historian has the duty to strip statements and deeds of uses to which later concerns had put them, of interpretations with which later purposes of a political party may have invested them, and of intentions for which strange requirements had utilized such words and actions.

In the churning, unfolding, shifting dynamism of history this transformation and reformation of deeds and words is a continuous process, and the biblical report is not free from its power. The words and deeds of Jesus come to us imbedded in the articulated concerns of the later career of the believing community, they are presented as germane to the predicaments and presuppositions and processes of the community that remembered and expanded them in *that community's* own interior and outer situation. Such a circumstance does not make recovery of meaning impossible; it certainly demands, however, the virtue of historical responsibility. Our first duty, then, if we would listen well, is to be as intelligent about this literature as we seek to be intelligent about Chaucer or Thucydides.

The second requirement for proper hearing is this: listen in a way appropriate to the nature of the discourse before you. One does not listen to the directions governing the use of drugs, for instance, in the same way one must listen to a short story or a poem. The language of a prescription is one-dimensional, non-allusive, purely designative. Any other kind of language would be positively dangerous. The intention is pure fact: two pills three times a day! The purpose of the statement is not to stimulate the imagination or to stir the soul; the purpose is to say how many pills to take at what intervals.

The parables of Jesus have a particular purpose and a style appropriate to them. They are dramatizations of the way the power of God bears upon the reality of humanity. And each one, could we know with complete certainty its placement and context, would disclose that an aspect of that power is laid over against a specific aspect of human life. Each one has a central intention, and even the incomplete range of our knowledge does not debar us from the recovery of it. What may debar us from such perception is that we allow ourselves to be seduced by the fascinating details so that we spatter our attention so broadly as to fail to ask and find what is the central thing that is being put forward. A point is being made; we must be careful to see all incidents, details, metaphors, etc., as instrumental to that point. If, for instance, in the parable of the workers in the vineyard we become concerned about how a modern labor union might react to the proposal of the vineyard owner as regards hours of work and the rate of pay we are off on the wrong, because unintended, track. The parable is not about economics or about justice. And the very strangeness of the earthly arrangement with the workers is instrumental to the heavenly point.

As then, so instructed, we listen to the parable read a few minutes ago we are to assume that it has a specific point and was directed to a recoverable situation. The recapitulation of the circumstances is a necessary preface to the point.

Jesus spoke, had his being, acted always from the central fact of the freedom and the

love of God. The freedom of God is precisely
the unfettered freedom of his love—his will
and work to restore all men to life in himself.

So majestic and absolute is this freedom
acting in love that it generates a devout blas-
phemy: it causes people, particularly religious people, to want to control the power
which controls them. So it was here. "One
Sabbath when he went to dine at the house
of a ruler who belonged to the Pharisees [the
strictest and most self-conscious guardians
of the religious tradition] they were watching
him." The verb *to watch* in this context does
not suggest an amiable, casual beholding; it
clearly suggests ". . . to watch maliciously, to
lie in wait for." The intention of the watching is to detect an improper move; its mood
is hostility.

The host and his guests had not to wait
very long. A man was there who had dropsy.
Jesus asked these regulators of the faith,
which presupposed a God whose nature was
to love in freedom, if it were lawful to heal
on the Sabbath. Caught in the old box
between the obviously right and the ordered
correct they were silent. Then Jesus healed
the man, let him go, and said to those who
"watched" him, "Which of you, having an ass
or an ox that has fallen into a well, will not
immediately pull him out on a Sabbath day?"
And they could not reply to this.

Now follows a little parable, just ahead of the one we are to consider in a moment, in which Jesus makes a point we would do well to get clear before we move on. The point is that things are not regarded by God as they are regarded by us. We have our canons of high and low, great and small, exalted and humble. The freedom and the love of God is a freedom and a love that makes a holy shambles of all of this. The purpose of God is simple, direct, undeviating: he wants people to join him at the table of his life and love, and if their calculating and protocol-loving arrangements get in the way he proceeds to sweep them aside.

For instance, "When you give a dinner do not invite friends or your brothers or your kinsmen or your rich neighbor, lest they also invite you in return, and you be repaid. But when you give a feast, invite the poor, the maimed, the lame, the blind, and you will be blessed, because they cannot repay you."

Here is a strange and shocking logic! Because they cannot, you have; because of nothing, everything. Because no conventional graciousness, immeasurable grace. This logic of holy love, this peculiar madness of grace was too fast for one of the men who heard this parable; it was just catching, as it were, the outside corner of his comprehension. So he did what we all do when we are

flustered by the sheer velocity of God's truth,
or disorganized by the clear or the swiftly
pure. He reached back into his inventory of
platitudes, found one of approximate size,
used it as a lid to contain this bubbling newness and vitality—"Blessed is he who shall eat
bread in the kingdom of God." Wrapped
cozily in a venerable and pious epigram the _Insulated_
man crawled back from the burning edge of _by the_
the gospel of God's freedom and love into the _his Truth_
familiar warmth of religion. _from God_

Now it is to that man and that action (and
to that man and to that action alive in all of
us) that our Lord tells the parable to which
we have been advancing. The record begins,
"But he said to him, . . ." clearly indicating
by the "but" that from the ground up a quite
new understanding had to be given. The
components of the long parable are as follows: A man proposed to give a great dinner
and to invite many persons. Two invitations
were issued to each: the first was to tell each
one that he was invited; the second, on the
day of the dinner, to announce that all was
now ready. The setting, we must remember, is
the orient. A festival dinner commonly was
built around a lamb roasted whole; the tim-
ing in such a case was approximate. When
the host was informed by servants that dinner was almost ready he dispatched other
servants to say to those invited, "Come, for

all is now ready." Each, however, had an excuse: a field to see, oxen to examine, a new bride to attend. The servant reported these excuses to his master.

So beguiling, because so familiar, is this excuse-making before the possibility of the holy that invades and pervades our lives, that it is quite natural that we should make a full stop at this point. This sullen unresponsiveness of human beings before God is so thumpingly actual a fact that we are sure we see in it the main point of the story. Each of us could do that, fill out each excuse with instant and shameful material from our own experience. And, having done that, we should leave this chapel clucking devoutly about our despicable recalcitrance before so gracious a God!

Will you rather reflect upon the possibility that so to do is not the point! To do that would be an exquisitely devout way to *miss* the point! To put the point *there* would be to make a moral house out of instrumental scaffolding. To put the point there is even worse than that; it is to pin our pity at the wrong place. We would then depart pitying God. Poor old God sitting there at his great table stuck with a burned roast!

Let us rather, as we say, get with it. The parable isn't finished. "So the servant came and reported this [the excuses] to his master.

Then the householder in anger said to his servant, 'Go out quickly to the streets and lanes of the city, and bring in the poor and maimed and blind and lame.' And the servant said, 'Sir, what you commanded has been done, and still there is room.' And the master said to the servant, 'Go out into the highways and hedges and compel people to come in, that my house may be filled.'"

Suddenly everything has shifted. The center of the parable is forcibly pulled away from people and their preoccupations and refusals, and the master of the dinner remains the master not only of the dinner but of the entire situation. He remains lord of his largess and of his purpose. That purpose is that people shall know the joy and the fellowship of their life's Lord, and he remains the Lord and executor of that purpose. People's refusals sadden him but they do not stop him; their sullenness angers him but it does not divert him. What he intends he accomplishes.

In these mad and sobering and revolutionary days we had better think about God like that. We are not, to be sure, disposed to think of the reality and the power of God in such a way. Collegiate reflections about God are anthropocentric: he is thought about in terms of *our* purposes, our existential traumas, our presuppositions, our needs. This parable has an utterly different twist. In the streets and

lanes of this world there is some peculiar and
unprecedented traffic-direction shaping up.
The culturally and otherwise accredited of
this world, having acted in sullen ways are
beholding movement among the blind, the
lame, the maimed, the poor. God wants people to know the joy and fullness of life in
himself—and this joy and fullness is not
unrelated to food and health and work to do.
And justice, above all. Long before Hellas
conceptualized a philosophy of justice, Israel
knew the magnificence and the endless burden of the righteousness that God requires.
"What does the Lord require of you, but to do
justice . . . ?"

If there be a Lord, and if he has requirements of people, and if his table of freedom-
in-love for the salvation of them involves the
earthly needs of their common humanity,
then there is a theology of history. And if
there is such a structured power and meaning and purpose, then the preoccupations of
human history (fields and cattle and wives in
marriage) can indeed advance or retard God's
purpose for his human family. But they cannot obliterate or change it.

And more! This parable suggests to us that
the first and most natural children of this
knowledge of the purpose of God are often
the first to deny or evade it. The churchly
beholders and bearers of this sharp vision,

the properly accredited voices of the message are today tempted to make a tame possession out of a passion, a mild loaf of religion out of this yeasty mass of godly dough. They are tempted to suppose that their ponderous ecclesiastical ways and decisions really settle the matter. Poor God there at his lonely table—he'll have to await the execution of his purposes for the unjustly treated Negro in Mississippi and Chicago and Angola until the historically accredited orderers of justice and the pace of its bestowal have determined who shall come to dinner.

We have a word to express how the gathering tension of a good story explodes in a final releasing statement; we call it the "punch line"! It is a requirement for our hearing of these stories from the gospels that tell the truth about how things really are between God and humans that we get the punch line at the right place.

In this story there is no doubt what that line is; it's at the very end. God wills many things, but not just many things in a general heap. There is an order in his will, a priority in his purpose. In these salubrious and successful days for popular Christianity it has become gauche to speak of the *wrath* of God. Love is fine to speak about; love is assumed to be a kind of disordered, irresolute, and generalized godly affection.

But this story makes very clear that there is a steady growl of anger at the heart of the holy, that the love of God for his human family has a hard and resolute intention. What that is, and certainty about God's will to see it through, comes out in the phrase, " . . . that my house may be filled." Not our house, but his house; not according to our specifications, but according to his will; not according to our preferences, but in ways appropriate to the awesome carelessness of his love.

2

The Role of Negation in Faith

NOTE: This sermon is illustrative of an effort that contemporary homiletics must occasionally make: to address head-on the situation that makes conventional homiletics ineffectual. The necessity of the effort does not, of course, guarantee its success.

What is here attempted is to analyze the interior components and moods of undergraduate negations. To the rejoinder that this is not a "proper" sermon one can only say that proper or not, clarity in the analysis of negations has the demonstrable effect of letting the student know that a cogent understanding of the reasons others reject the gospel is itself a kind of invitation to what the preacher has to say!

Mr. T. S. Eliot concludes one of his essays with the comment that it is the destiny of some periods of history not to shape new forms of affirmation but only so to labor that some things be not forgotten. It may be that in philosophy, religion, and in all human endeavors we are the children of such a necessity. So vast has been the demolition, so radical the shift of interest, and so astounding the velocity with which we have been thrust into a world in which the solutions require wholeness of strategic vision that our embarrassment is deepened by the very insouciance with which we order our learned fragments. Philosophy is making recondite adjustments in its venerable machinery. Art is creatively fumbling for a form among a spattered plethora of points of vision—celebrating its own integrity by honest documentation of the fact that it finds nothing integral to celebrate. And much of Christian theology, having gazed wistfully at the corrosion of its once substantial instruments for inquiry into the meaning of truth, faith, purpose, will, and end, is carrying on an extramarital affair with the personality sciences. That this affair is carried on in clinically antiseptic and well-lighted circumstances does not abolish the fact that wife and children are waiting in the old house.

And when one is engaged, as I regularly am, in an effort to transmit and reinterpret the terms and affirmations of the catholic Christian tradition to students in a university one becomes aware that the search for a place even to begin talking is a formidable one. If the teacher in his personal life were disengaged from all that contributes to this confusion the way out would present peculiar but quite formal problems. But when the pegs in the teacher's own mind, experience, and contemporary feeling for life are loosened and all arattle, the formal bewilderment becomes a positive panic.

But one must, nevertheless, begin. If one cannot begin with a consensus of affirmations, then one must begin with a consensus of negations; if not with an explication of a time's "yes," then with an analysis of the forms of its "no," and a sensitive search for meanings perhaps covertly alive in the very passion of the proclamation of no meaning. We must make an effort to catalog forms of negation, bring into clear statement the etiology of the no which men speak to the Christian story of God's coming to humanity in Jesus Christ.

First, the negation of no concern. Not a negation, that is to say, which is the verdict of a judgment but a negation that has not operated at the level of judgment at all. A person's life may be so directed toward, filled with, contentedly unfolded among the sheer operational activities of local and immediate existence that issues having the dimensions of an ultimate concern simply do not swim in that person's pond at all! Religious institutions regularly tell themselves that there are no such people, preaching proceeds on the assumption that such an atrophy of what would seem to be a general human longing for large meanings has really not occurred, and says of the situation what our Lord said of the daughter of Jairus, "The maid is not dead, but sleepeth." But the theologian who operates on the assumption that people cannot actually die to ultimacy but only become temporarily stultified, stupefied, fat, or frivolous, have to weight the quiet apostolic judgment in the fourth chapter of the Epistle to the Ephesians, a literal translation of which is, "Now I insist and protest in the Lord that you give up living like Pagans, with their minds unable to get ahold of anything, darkened in their under-standing, cut off from the life of God by the sheer stupidity of an ossified heart." Paul saw this as a frightening possibility. The contem-porary person knows it as an actuality.

Second, the negation of instrumental inadequacy. By this phrase I mean that the terms and the power of the Christian story may be adjudged so far to transcend any effectual and just embodiment in statement, creed, institutional form, or personal actual-ization in spirit that they are negated even as a dream is negated. In the strict sense this turning away is not a negation at all; it may, indeed, be a profound affirmation. But its practical effect, if unattended by effects appropriate to what is beheld ever so fleetingly, is negative.

When, for an instance, one ponders the size, character, and complexity of the moral predicaments and possibilities elaborated in Joseph Conrad's novel *Nostromo,* and watches worked out with superb artistic precision the problem of the actualization of the will to social good, and is made aware in the process of the ambiguity intrinsic to any fusion of vision and accomplishment, then one recognizes the truth of this type of negation.

When Conrad's protagonist surveys the strange outcome, the outer improvement of the conditions of life actually generating an inner recalcitrance to the larger possibilities of spirit, he says with sadness, "The better good will come after us." The envisioned better good can only be stated in terms drawn from the Christian story—repentance, expiation, regeneration, forgiveness, and faith (and Conrad does not hesitate to use such terms) but the negation, while complete, is instrumental. The good is not repudiated, nor is faith in its ultimacy dead. What is dead is the confidence that humanity has the constancy or wisdom to translate such a good into effectual form. Here, as in so many negations in the contemporary literature of moral analysis, the negation is a kind of reflex to a subterranean affirmation, an affirmation made, to be sure, in terms appropriate to art rather than to theology—but an affirmation inconceivable apart from the penetration of the whole of Western culture by the powers and promises and judgments of the Christian gospel.

Third, negation as a protective device for the fragility of such apprehensions as have not sufficiently matured for either private acknowledgement or public exposure. That this type of negation should characterize many students is not strange, for the very ecology in which the story of grace has for centuries been transmitted to our childhood, richly replete with its appropriate images and potent with non-cognitive referents—this ecology has been utterly disrupted in contemporary American culture. It is one thing to tell a student that the story of Jacob and the angel is somewhat more than a celebrated wrestling match; it is quite another thing to make the point to an eroded topsoil that does not contain the figure of Jacob! Without images language cannot address humanity in the depths of its humanity; the image of Dante's Beatrice does not disclose its positive religious depth save to the one experience of the penultimate loves of earth has broken open to the possibility of the poet's noble closing:

> As one
> Who versed in geometric lore, would fain
> Measure the circle; and, through pondering
>   long
> And deeply, that beginning which he needs,
> Finds not; e'en such as I—
>
> Here vigour fail'd the tow'ring fantasy:
> But yet the will roll'd onward, like a wheel
> In the even motion, by the Love impell'd,
> That moves the sun in heav'n and all the
> stars.[1]

It is not while beguiled by the sufficiency of empirical fact, or soon, that the protective negation will sing quiet praises within or outwardly admit to a dawning apprehension of a fresh and astounding new possibility for faith.

Fourth, negation as the mind's violent repudiation of prudential reasons for offering a non-prudential good. It is a tribute to many an undergraduate mind that it has smelled a large and very dead rat when the holiest and most general claims of the Christian faith have been supported with reasons of the most unholy, local, and prudential sort. One must be careful how one expounds the text

"Blessed is the people whose God is the Lord." For if one promises such blessings in terms of an enhancement of happiness, security, peace, the integrated personality, or proposes a guaranteed correlation between national piety and the gross national product, one is not only promising what grace has never promised to deliver, but is transforming grace itself into a religious device for the achievement of that sufficiency of the self which grace calls hell, and from which it comes to deliver man. There is relation between piety and a steady national purpose, but when piety is commended in order that uncriticized purposes may be steadied on their course, a good has been affirmed by such arguments of usefulness as to suggest a confusion of order in the mind's integrity. And when this confusion begets intellectual revulsion, and revulsion begets negation, the properly accredited angels of God do not weep for the lost; they are more likely to applaud the logical negation. For it reveals a healthy, quick suspicion, which, while indeed no affirmation, discloses a mind that knows the difference between an affirmation as big as life and a gimmick as old as Luther's bitter epigram "Man seeks himself in everything—even in God!"

Fifth, negation as the persistence of a conditioned reflex whose history is past seductions now understood to have been false simplicities. Just as fingers once burned explore more cautiously, and hope once crushed is less quick to spring again, so the mind remembers almost with shame its own history. A huge and rose simplicity was beguilingly offered in the form of the Christian story and the mind went out like an ingenuous child to meet it. But it was all a seduction. The gallant promises either crumpled up in the hard clutch of need or became mockingly simple symbols of childhood as they retreated before the dawning of ambiguity in the moral intelligence.

It is hard to know how to assign responsibility for this fact of American religious life: that the maturation of simple ideas in response to deepening complexities of life which has marked our political, social, and literary history has not been attended with a parallel maturation in our administration of the Christian story. We seem resolved to keep that story encysted in its elementary terms. This resolution seems to have two grounds: first, we have a tradition of piety which is offended by the suggestion that the story is a tough, penetrating, hard doctrine whose theater is the dark dreads, tormenting anxieties, and constructive demands of life. We often seek to honor its nostalgically remembered service to our wide-eyed past by keeping it wrapped in such tissues as wrapped it when it first came to us. And, second, the pragmatic tradition in the American common life has so powerfully squeezed the story to a flat, monodimensional and predominantly moral magnitude that is simply not available for decent residence in the multi-roomed house of the mind. While, to be sure, a part of the fault for this must properly be laid at the door of religious institutions and voices—for they have remained silent under the peculiar apologia of the politicos that faith is functional to civic virtue and solidarity—an even larger responsibility belongs to public education. When it becomes an unchallenged dogma that education is for life in a democracy, then meanings which are not transparently instrumental toward *that* end are either not beheld or untransmitted. Both Nathaniel Hawthorne and Walt Whitman had a sense for the challenge of the Christian story to all social idolatries and moral uncandor, but in my life, matched by the experience of many another, it required the suspicion that Hawthorne was talking about something more than New England antiquities and idiosyncrasies, and Whitman something more than the illimitable geography of the American continent to find that out!

For some people maturation toward affirmation proceeds by the path of negations;

for a total proposal for total meaning can bring such persons to the point of ultimate decision only if negations are confronted and made to do battle with the absurdity of existence. But our common national history, daily confirmed by the pieties of our leaders, seldom gets beyond the dubious and irrelevant assumption that "moral fiber" can be manufactured by appeal.

Sixth, and by all means the most profound form of negation, is a protest of affirmative nature against what seem to be, and are indeed often presented as, the limiting, denigrating, and sterilizing claims of grace. There is a sense in which all vitalities of grace do operate to limit, denigrate, and sterilize. This questioning of all penultimate values belongs to the concept of God, as that concept is permitted freedom to create its own categories in the classical theological tradition. To speak of the omnipotence of God is a meaningful statement only when this *omni* and this *potens* stand over against humanity's limitation and powerlessness in ultimate things. That is not a religious but a logical statement. To speak of the goodness of God is a meaningful statement not as a continuity extrapolated from the relentless ambiguity of all human goodness, but of a goodness of such a purity that only by its logical opposition-role in the story of humanity can its intention be clarified. To speak of the eternity of God is a meaningful statement only if its intention be filled in a negative way over against the mutable facts of a human life.

All of this is but a way of saying that all that humans can know of God in some periods is the way in which they cannot know God. God's power tells him only the negative fact of their powerlessness; God's goodness tells them of, and gives the lure to, the infuriating admixture of good and self-seeking; God's eternity tells them only of his mutability and passingness.

And therefore, negation of God may be for some a kind of necessary cathartic, a necessary operation of the mind which must take place in order to bring to decisive clarity precisely what is involved in the affirmation of God. The negation of the transcendent is often the moment of taking out one's membership in the human race because the affirmation of divinity is a perilous thing for one if it be made in ignorance of the magnificence of humanity. The dominical word "Love not the world" is a perilous thing to say to one who does not know the world, or who despises it, or walks through it blinding one's eyes or holding one's nose. The freedom of faith in God cannot receive its full, gracious scope until one has joined the exulting company of one's fellows, and cried with them, "O brave new world, that hath such people in it." The world has its good, and affirmations of eternity and divinity that do not live within and educate the mind through this human good are liable to be febrile and insecure. By these goods is not meant the comfort-supplying possibilities of success controlling a fantastic technology. But rather this: the incalculable endowments available to the life of reason, effort, attention, discipline; vision and promises of private and common life awaiting the application of bold programs, adequate control of social power, appropriate procedures for common good, refined instruments of law and government in order to justice.

There are some who have to come within hailing distance of the vision of the kingdom of God by denying its historical past-meanings, expanding denial by vigorous participation in the kingdom of humanity, and learning there afresh that this denying one is precisely the creature who relentlessly asks the question about God!

It is clear to me that one does not have to postulate God or grace in order to affirm humanity; that one does not have to affirm the eternal to protest against destructive fall-out in the human temporal; that one does not have to affirm the holy to love truth, serve the light, love the multiform lavishness of existence, serve the age. Along the way to grace one may have to pass through the pagan affirmation, tough in resolution and tender in substance, which repudiates grace in the name of nature when it cries:

> Wilt thou yet take all, Galilean? but these
> thou shalt not take,
> The laurel, the palms and the paean, the
> breasts of the nymphs in the brake; . . .[2]

When shall we come to understand that grace, properly understood, cannot repudiate nature! For while nature, hurt, self-incurved, meaningless in the grip of humanity's sin, and used by humans as material for their idolatry, is not a preacher of the gospel of Jesus Christ, it is yet a creation of God and a theater of his grace. The Galilean, to continue Swinburne's poem, does not wish to "take all" in the sense of taking away or repudiating all; he wishes that all may be seen as God's gift and place and presence. As such the world has its laurels, its palms, and its paeans, but all of these are ours in a fresh-gifted way: "For all things are yours, and ye are Christ's, and Christ is God's."

Many and subtle and sometimes jagged are the ways one is led by the Spirit of God to make the Christian confession. One of these, historically, has been the *via nega-tiva,* the way of negation. And it just might be that the swollen idolatries of our epoch represent this way as the necessary way for millions of disenchanted children of once vibrant but now vacated meanings. The form of the contemporary negation can be seen as operating in a way that actually negates the negation; it is a stirring at a level of existence-in-passion that, in a negative way, is opening a new possibility for a fresh decision about the reality of grace for humans in this world.

There is a considerable body of evidence in modern poetry, short story, novel, drama, and in painting that the tough dialectic of the *imago dei* is about its deep-down indestructible business. This dialectic has a tactic with the idolatrous human; the repudiated *yes* of grace reappears as a possibility precisely in the *no* expanded to its end; the blessing of the limit of selfhood is exposed in the vacuous dream of limitlessness; the reality of the biblical word that one is given selfhood always in God's created garden with other selves is being rediscovered in the exacerbation of the private self.

In the Gospels this negative wrench or intrusion of the positive has the generality of a parable. Nicodemus must so negate all that he means by being that only the absurd "You must be born again" is violent enough to carry the point. The ruler must negate all that it means to be human, i.e., his definition of himself in the human-relationship ("All these things have I done from my youth") in order to be justified in the God-relationship, and thus be driven to a right relationship by way of negation.

Negation, finally, is not a phase of faith, or simply prolegomenon to it; it may remain an element in the inmost character of faith. The no to grace is not only the existential occasion for the perception of it as a possibility: it may continue as steady accompaniment to the mature life in grace. Because a man is reported in the Gospels to have cried, "I believe; help my unbelief!" we have no reason to conclude, and every reason to know, that this ambivalence is not always annihilated by faith. It is rather tightened and made more pressing. In Søren Kierkegaard's meditations on the Johannine phrase, "sickness unto death," this fact of the persistence of doubt as constitutive of faith is worked out with a psychological finesse that is relentless, and of almost demonic delicacy. A sickness is structural to life, and more acute to the eyes of faith than to humane eyes not thus determined. But there is a difference between a sickness which is unto life, and a sickness which is, indeed, unto death. And the name for that invincible health that stands steady within all sickness is faith in God.

3

The View from Mount Nebo

NOTE: One is sometimes called upon so to preach as to correct an imbalance, violently to attack an understanding of the Christian faith which, if not corrected, permits people to reject an authentic Christian faith because they reject a caricature.

The following sermon was preached to such a situation. A summer camp under presumably Christian auspices was manned by several hundred students, and they assembled each Sunday for an hour of worship. The prevailing ethos of the camp was Christian—experiential, sentimental. Personal testimonies around an emotion-stirring campfire were a regular evening feature.

For many students this procedure was normal, authentic, an accustomed way. For others it was abnormal, inauthentic, strange. But the students who rejected the custom felt that they were somehow outside the orbit of normal Christian experience. And the feeling troubled them. This sermon was addressed to the outsiders.

And Moses went up from the plains of Moab to Mount Nebo, to the top of Pisgah, which is opposite Jericho. And the LORD showed him all the land, Gilead as far as Dan, all Naphtali, the land of Ephraim and Manasseh, all the land of Judah as far as the Western Sea, the Negeb, and the Plain, that is, the valley of Jericho the city of palm trees, as far as Zoar. And the LORD said to him, "This is the land of which I swore to Abraham, to Isaac, and to Jacob, 'I will give it to your descendents.' I have let you see it with your eyes, but you shall not go over there." So Moses the servant of the LORD died there in the land of Moab, according to the word of the Lord, and he buried him in the valley in the land of Moab opposite Bethpeor; but no man knows the place of his burial to this day. Moses was a hundred and twenty years old when he died; his eye was not dim, nor his natural force abated. And the people of Israel wept for Moses in the plains of Moab thirty days; then the days of weeping and mourning for Moses were ended.

And Joshua the son of Nun was full of the spirit of wisdom, for Moses had laid his

hands upon him; so the people of Israel
obeyed him, and did as the LORD *had com-*
manded Moses. And there has not arisen a
prophet since in Israel like Moses, whom the
LORD *knew face to face, none like him for all*
the signs and the wonders which the LORD *sent*
him to do in the land of Egypt, to Pharaoh
and to all his servants and to all his land, and
for all the mighty power and all the great and
terrible deeds which Moses wrought in the
sight of all Israel.

—*Deuteronomy 34*

One should not oversimplify the Christian
doctrine of the Holy Spirit. That doctrine
declares that faith is a work of God's Spirit,
that it is God alone who can cause one in
full personal decision to make the Christian
confession.

But sometimes we so speak, or more often
sing, of the work of the Holy Spirit as to
reduce to a single and simple way the enormous variety of ways the Holy Spirit accomplishes his work. One such oversimplification
is celebrated in the hymn that has a melancholy popularity among many young peo-
ples' groups.

Blessed assurance, Jesus is mine.
O what a foretaste of glory divine.

What this hymn suggests is that nothing Christian is authentic until and unless it has become a blessed assurance in some specifiable, warm, pervasive, and crucial experience.

This assumption points to a truth, and it encourages an error. The truth is that a person is an organic whole, integral, and that there is a continuity between outside and inside, appearance and reality. There is a momentum between confession and total being. But the error is the assumption that Christian faith is normally identical with what has been confirmed in that way. That assumption is not only erroneous; it is dangerous. For it invites the mind to reduce the Christian pronouncement and claim to those elements which have been certified in the heat of one's individual experience. Such an error is both reductive and perverting for it shrinks and twists the magnificence, the scope, and the objectivity of Christian fact to the dimension of personal and largely temperamental endowments. It tempts us to hang the reality of God, the compass of his demands, the scope of biblical and theological meaning, upon a febrile nail: the warmth and immediacy of a feeling of blessed assurance.

This subjectivizing of the Christian faith presents problems for us. Instead of speaking of these abstractly I have chosen to speak of one such problem as I know it concretely. For

some years I was dean of students in a theological seminary of my church and had fre-
quently to talk with students who came to
me disturbed because their sense of vocation
was not as strong, or as inwardly certified, as
they felt it ought to be if they were going to
be ordained ministers of the Christian gospel.
They said, "I believe the gospel and that one
ought to preach it. But how do I know that
this task is for me? I don't have that interior
confirmation whereby I can have a sense of
absolute certainty in my vocation as a
Christian minister."

I have sometimes been able to be of help
to such students because I have walked and
walk that same rope. I feel the same absence
of this "blessed assurance" in my own life. I,
too, make uncertified postulation of the
Christian faith, uncertified, that is, by auxil-
iary feelings that are supposed somehow to
make it "more true." In my experience in
teaching and preaching the story of the
Christian faith I recall an instance in my own
parish when I was preaching straight through
Philippians. I did pretty well through the first
part of the first chapter. This part is historical and reportorial; I could simply say that
this is what happened to Paul, and this is the
way he responded. Then I came to the verse
that really separates the men from the boys:
verse 21 in the first chapter, "For to me to

live is Christ, and to die is gain." I had to begin my sermon by saying, "I must declare to you something this morning that I do not know anything about." My job was not to say, "This is true, and I can testify that it is true," because I would have been a liar to say that. I had not yet come to the point (and I have not yet come to it, either) where I can say, "If I die today it is all right with me. For me to die is gain." I do not have the gifts of grace whereby I can say this. My duty, instead, is to say that the man who said the other true things in the first chapter of Philippians did not suddenly turn into a phony when he said this! "I don't know that this is so, but Saint Paul knew that it was so" was a proper statement. My duty was to say that grace has this magnificent possibility, it *can* do that to a person, and for Paul, it did. He could then say that "if they take me to Rome and cut my head off next week, or whether I return to you at Philippi is no longer the fundamental issue."

I wish I had so rich and gallant a gift. But my duty is not to reduce the message to the size of what I have or have not; it is proper sometimes to declare what one does not know.

But is this just my problem? Is it just my pilgrimage? I think not. There are thousands of students today to whom the Christian faith must be declared as if they, too, stood in that

same position. And it is for that reason that I
have chosen the title, "The View from Mt.
Nebo." It suggests different perspectives for
looking in upon things. There are many
mountains in the Bible: Mt. Hermon, Mt.
Zion, Mt. Calvary. But there is that other
peak, Mt. Nebo. And I ask you to regard this
peak as a kind of symbol by which to eluci-
date a way of standing within the problem of
"blessed assurance."

Think of three perspectives from which one
can envision and begin to talk about the
Christian faith. First, the perspective from
within. Most talk about Christianity does, and
should, proceed from this warm, immediate
perspective from within the body of the people of God in Christ. They speak out of and in
the language of this beloved community
which knows what it means to have been
redeemed from the insecurities and egocen-
tricities of perilous life. They are firmly held
by the action of God, speak of it with adoration, understanding, enthusiasm. The great
objective story of Christianity has been reen-
acted within their own experience in such a
way that an outer nativity at Bethlehem has
become an inner nativity whereby they know
a new birth. An incarnation *there* has
wrought a strange new person *here*. A death
in the great story is now interpreted to be a
death of self from which one rises in answer

to the outer resurrection to a newness of life in every moment of one's breathing existence. This perspective from within, which I see and partly understand, is always the first central perspective for declaring the Christian story. Christ is love, and joy, peace, hope; and all these gifts are given by the Holy Ghost. They are, as Paul says, "the fruits of the Spirit."

As your preacher this morning, it is only honest to say that I have never known fully that kind of life within the full, warm power of that faith for whose declaration I am an ordained minister. The very term, "Christian experience," as generally understood, has small meaning for me. I have not seen any burning bushes. I have not pounded at the door of God's grace with the passion of a Martin Luther. John Wesley's "strangely warmed" heart at Aldersgate Street—this is not my street. I have not the possibility to say of the Christian faith what many honest people have said about it. But I have come to see that to declare as a gift of God what I do not fully possess is, nevertheless, a duty of obedience. Is the opulence of the grace of God to be measured by my inventory? Is the great catholic faith of nineteen centuries to be reduced to my interior dimensions? Are the arching lines of the gracious "possible" to be pulled down to the little spurts of my personal compass? Is the great heart of the reality of God to speak in only the broken accent that I can follow after? No. That ought not to be. Therefore, one is proper and right when one sometimes talks of things one doesn't know all about. In obedience to the bigness of the story which transcends one's own apprehension, one may do this.

A second perspective is the perspective from without. The first perspective is characterized by participation, the second by detachment. The view from without has not the same legitimacy or the same kind of power as the view from within. But it has, nevertheless, its own power, its own function, and it addresses students of today with a particular kind of velocity. It is primarily critical, reportorial, or, as the student in sciences would call it, phenomenological. It asks what it means to be a Christian. What does this community called Christian intend, whence did it come, what did it affirm as it came into history, how is this community constituted, what does it declare about the nature of truth and reality, how has it embodied its affirmations in cultural-historical institutions and in ethics?

Now that is perhaps not a very exciting way to be a Christian. But I should like to suggest that you think of what the Christian community owes to the quiet people who view from this second perspective. These are people who never raise their voices in declaration or declamation, seldom praise in public, never offer moving testimonials. Who knows what goes on in the hearts of people who lack the grace of adoration, of passion, of immediate "blessed assurance," who lack full knowledge of God, who must live out their lives in hard, dutiful obedience to lesser, cooler graces because their lives are unattended by the hotter ones? These people's Christian lives are given, rather, to discernment, critical work, the effort to achieve a precise description of what is really involved in becoming and being a Christian.

I once studied for some months in a German university. One of my professors was a great teacher of preaching. This man could not preach, and he never tried to. He was too honest to claim to have what the Bible talks about and promises. But he knew what the biblical promise was, he knew that when the Bible talks of the kingdom of God it does not mean habitual piety, puritan mores, better homes and gardens, middle-class respectability, soul sweetness and body cleanliness, inoffensive community acceptability. He knew that when he was talking about redemption, salvation, sin, faith, grace he was talking about huge and clear realities. He would not permit us to palm off phony realities in the name of these. He knew that, whether he had the gift of these realities or not, they do constitute what it means to be a Christian.

The third perspective is that of many of us who are students. It has a peculiar pathos, a peculiar toughness, honesty, and promise for the days that lie ahead. It is the perspective of many today who do not know if they ought to call themselves Christians at all, but who are saddened in their feeling of being outside the Christian company.

It is this third perspective which is suggested by our lesson from Deuteronomy. Will you recall the scripture lesson from Deuteronomy which talks about Moses on Mt. Nebo in the land of Moab. Recall what you know about Moses. This man was a strong, spiritual, and faithful man.

He was a strong man. He steadfastly pointed with all the force of his massive personal power to the will of God for his people. He kept their ears open to God, he kept their faces turned toward their destiny, and he kicked their reluctant feet along the road to their heavenly possession. Michelangelo's great actualization of the figure of Moses is not wrong: that awesome figure is all the trouble and the Exodus and the hard wilderness of Israel portrayed in stone.

Moses was a spiritual man. He was determined by the Spirit that called him to live his life under a certain discipline and task. Spiritual does not mean to be wrapped in a kind of holy gas which becomes ignited around testimonial campfires. For Moses it meant to have his will and decisions determined by the Spirit of God. He knew that God had a will for his people and that a human's spirit was to be subjected to that great Spirit. He was, therefore, a lawgiver, that is, the voice of the Spirit of God who constituted this particular people and gave them particular laws. Moses would never let them forget that—and Deuteronomy is his monument.

Moses was a faithful man. He obeyed even when he did not understand. He held to the command. He obeyed the vision in Egypt, in the wilderness, on Mt. Sinai, and even on Mt. Nebo. There is where we see him in this lesson.

Moses on Mt. Nebo is a man in the situation of many of us who feel we must confess and serve a faith whose gifts to us are not given with all the opulence we might desire, and in whose lives the very gifts of grace do not control us who are the declarers of these same gifts. Here is a perspective from which many a man must view the life of the church, the tradition, and the pathos of his own position. Moses saw clearly, but he could not enter into what he saw. The poorest child of that people who entered into the land of promise had what Moses, who led them to the land, could never have. Moses had sight without actuality; he had knowledge without possession. Moses knew more about what Israel meant than most people in Israel. But he died outside the land.

At this particular moment in our religious and intellectual history the perspective from Mt. Nebo is a necessary one. It is good for many of today's college students to see the man who from Nebo's peak was yet strong, spiritual, faithful. For students are being invited to sit in the cozy rooms of religious togetherness, and seek violently after "commitment"—a kind of contemporary term for the older blessed assurance. And many of them can't bring it off. The conventional standard psychological equipment of blessed assurance has not been given them. They are critical, historically self-conscious, they know a thing or two about the vast variety of stages on the way to the Christian confession, and they are not disposed to indulge in these too-quick oversimplifications which university studies have warned them against.

It is at such a moment that the perspective from Mt. Nebo may be useful to us. The people of Mt. Nebo are the obedient children of both participation and detachment. They know and they do not know fully. They participate because they come from the tradition and tuition of the faith, and have been so deeply formed by it that they cannot escape its terms, its claims, its ethics. And they do not want to. They know the power and the good of the God relationship in all things: they know it to be true, and rich, and free. They want to be open to the renewing power of the Holy, but at the same time, while they participate, they do not fully enter. Their participation is a kind of "hurt" participation: they do not possess those gifts of the Spirit—love, joy, peace, hope— which would permit them without a kind of sardonic footnote to sing "Blessed assurance, Jesus is mine." Nevertheless, they want to affirm those very gifts as being a possibility of God for the world.

Now from the inside, for many of us tormented by this precise perspective, this means that we must sometimes envision with the mind what the heart cannot yet confirm, must see and affirm with clear intellectual sight what we have not been given the grace to celebrate in actual life. And yet, how great is our debt to those *without* grace who out of the passion of their poverty sing the songs of grace!

Think, for instance, of Søren Kierkegaard, that great Christian man, who out of a loveless love has written of love with excruciating penetration. Just as the hungry talk of food, or the thirsty of water, so does this mordant man who loved hopelessly write of human love with a penetration and a passion which few have ever equaled. Here is a strange fact: precision in knowledge and statement may have two mothers, and they are in contradiction. There is a precision which is born of knowledge: the clear, joyous precision of the insider who lives completely with the faith. St. Francis had it. John Calvin had it. And there is the other precision: the precision begotten of deprivation, the tormented precision of vision without gift. There are some in the Christian tradition who have described the reality of certain graces because they lived their lives, not within the vitality and fragrance of these graces, but because they stood outside longingly looking in and described with tormented precision what they saw. They are the people of Mt. Nebo who see what their feet cannot touch, and out of negation forge those clear descriptions which then become the dear possession of the children of the land. These are the people who in sheer thought forge ideas in longing that others affirm in quiet and unquestioning possession. Pathos gives a toughness that affirmation profits by.

Now, you will tell me, faith without works is dead, and you are quite right. The people of Mt. Nebo know this with an excruciating clarity that the calm quoters of the passage seldom know. And out of their poverty they fashion the only possible gift they can bring to the faith—a clarity given to the bereft that enables others to know and to find.

On the peak of Nebo, between participation without substance and detachment without peace they add their astringent voice to the song of faith. Without the lean people of Nebo the people on Mt. Zion are always tempted to become fat. There is a beatitude in the New Testament which reads: "Blessed are they that hunger and thirst, . . . for they shall be filled." I would suggest to this disconsolate student generation that in the long history of the intellectual life of the church and having a poignant force in these confusing days when the very nature of Christian truth and its relation to the world is being refashioned, a second little beatitude may be wrought out for our comfort in a lesser and a stranger way: "Blessed also are they that hunger and thirst without being filled." For just to hunger and thirst, and to know without settling for it, that you *do* hunger and thirst, is given a kind of negative benediction. Hunger, unabated, is a kind of testimony to the reality of good. To want to have may become a strange kind of having.

4

The Care of the Earth[1]

A sermon may move from idea to fulfillment in various and sometimes strange
ways. It may be useful as an introduction to
the theme of this sermon to say how that
happened in the writing of it.

In April of last year I read a poem in the
New Yorker magazine; the poet is Mr.
Richard Wilbur. What the poet was saying
struck and stuck for several obvious reasons.
Beneath the quite clear apprehensions that
float about just under the surface of our
minds there is a root apprehension that
churns deep down at the center. It is vague,
but it is also relentless and undismissable.
And the poet's words interest this inarticulate
anxiety, stop it cold, give it a "local habita-
tion and a name." The substance of this anxiety is common to us all, and it is heavy. It is
the peculiar function of the poet sometimes
to say out loud and with resonant clarity

what we all would wish to say had we the dark music and the language.

The substance is this: annihilating power is in nervous and passionate hands. The stuff is really there to incinerate the earth—and the certainty that it will not be used is not there.

Nor have we anodyne to hush it up or power to run away from it. We can go skiing with it, trot off to Bermuda with it, push it down under accelerated occupation with the daily round, pour bourbon over it, or say our prayers—each according to our own tactic and disposition. But it goes along, survives, talks back.

Not in abstract proposition or dramatic warnings but in powerful, earthy images the poet makes his point. The point is single, simple, and absolute: humanity's selfhood hangs upon the persistence of the earth, *her* dear known and remembered factualness is the matrix of the self.

When you come, as you soon must,
    to the streets of our city,
Mad-eyed from stating the obvious,
Not proclaiming our fall but begging us
In God's name to have self-pity,

Spare us all word of the weapons, their
    force and range,
The long numbers that rocket the mind;

Our slow, unreckoning hearts will be left
   behind,
Unable to fear what is too strange.

Nor shall you scare us with talk of the death
   of the race.
How should we dream of this place without
   us—
The sun mere fire, the leaves untroubled
   about us,
A stone look on the stone's face?

Speak of the world's own change. Though
   we cannot conceive
Of an undreamt thing, we know to our cost
How the dreamt cloud crumbles, the vines
   are blackened by frost,
How the view alters. We could believe,

If you told us so, that the white-tailed deer
   will slip
Into perfect shade, grown perfectly shy,
The lark avoid the reaches of our eye,
The jack-pine loose its knuckled grip

On the cold ledge, and every torrent burn
As Xanthus once, its gliding trout
Stunned in a twinkling. What should we be
   without
The dolphin's arc, the dove's return,

These things in which we have seen
   ourselves and spoken?
Ask us, prophet, how we shall call
Our natures forth when that live tongue is
   all
Dispelled, that glass obscured or broken,

In which we have said the rose of our love
   and the clean
Horse of our courage, in which beheld
The singing locust of the soul unshelled,
And all we mean or wish to mean.

Ask us, ask us whether with the wordless
   rose
Our hearts shall fail us; come demanding
Whether there shall be lofty or long
   standing
When the bronze annals of the oak-tree
   close.[2]

By sheer force of these lines my mind was
pushed back against the wall and forced to
ask: Is there anything in our western religious
tradition as diagnostically penetrating as that
problem, as salvatory as that predicament?

Out of these back-to-wall reflections I
therefore ask your attention to several statements that seem to me alone deep and
strong enough to make adequate sense.

These statements have in common this: they deal with the *enjoyment* of things and the *uses* of things. And together they add up to a proposition: delight is the basis of right use.

The first statement is the celebrated answer to the first question in the Westminster catechism. No one will question the velocity with which this answer gets to the point or that the point is worth getting at! The question is: what is the chief end of man? The answer: to glorify God and enjoy him forever!

The first verb, to glorify, is not primarily intellectual. It does not concern itself with the establishment of the existence of God, or with a description of his nature. The verb is not aesthetic either. It is not concerned to declare that God is good or beautiful, or propose that it is a fair thing to worship God. Nor is it hortatory, that is, it does not beat us over the head with admonitions about our duty to God.

The very "to glorify" is exclusively and utterly religious! The verb comes from the substantive "glory": and that term designates that God is and has and wills within himself; it announces the priority, the ineffable majesty, the sovereign power and freedom of the holy. Glory, that is to say, is what God is and does out of himself; and when we use the term for what we do in response, that response is given and engendered by his glory.

The priority-in-God, and the proper work of this verb may be illustrated by its function in the sixth chapter of the book of Isaiah. The young prophet, rich and eager in his expectations of the new king, Uzziah, is stunned when the king dies. He goes into the temple, and then comes the vision of the glory of whose ineffable power the face of the king is but the reflection.

> In the year that King Uzziah died I saw the Lord sitting upon a throne, high and lifted up; and his train filled the temple. Above him stood the seraphim; each had six wings: with two he covered his face, and with two he covered his feet, and with two he flew. And one called to another and said:
> "Holy, holy, holy is the Lord of hosts;
>   the whole earth is full of his glory."[3]

The glory is the light the holy gives off. The earth is a theater of the glory; it is rich with the ineffable glory because God, the holy one, has made it.

The holy is a numinous and absolute word. It is not contained within other categories; it is a category. The holy both evokes and demands thoughts, but it is a misunderstanding to assume that thoughts can contain the glory and the holy. The holy certainly has the effect that Professor Rudolph Otto in his great work, *The Idea of the Holy,* calls *mysterium tremendum et fascinosum*— but there is an unseizable plus to the term that eludes even the image-making genius of the Jews.

The holy invites prayer, but rejects such an understanding of prayer as would make prayer a tool for working upon the holy, a device for making the holy disposable by humanity. The holy demands service, but no service adds up to a responding equivalent— just as in our human love one serves the beloved but never affirms one's service to be the measure of love.

The chief end of man is, then, to glorify God, to let God *be* God, to understand and accept his life in ways appropriate to the imperial, holy singularity of God. The meaning of this has, to be sure, ethical, psychological, even political implications. But the center is categorically religious.

But this statement about God and humanity, thus elevated, tough, and absolute, is conjoined in the catechism with a concluding phrase, "and enjoy him forever." The juxtaposition of commands to glorify and to enjoy is on several grounds startling to our generation. To enjoy is a strange thing, that is to say, to do about the holy God before whom even the seraphim do hide their faces. This joining of the *holy,* which is what God is, with *joy,* which designates what humanity is to have and do in him—this juxtaposition, in that it is startling to us, says a good deal about modern American understanding of the Christian faith. How it has come about that we are startled by what our ancestors joined together without batting an eye is a matter we cannot now go into, but only observe it and ask after its significance. For we may have missed something. If the gravity of the glorification of the holy and the blithe humanness of "enjoy him forever" seem strange, our churches in the very form of their buildings may be partly to blame. There is the clean, shadowless, and antiseptic colonial, the monumental melancholy of the Romanesque and Gothic adaptations—bereft of the color and ornament which in other lands are so devoutly joined in these forms. Our traditional churches affirm a heavy kind of solemnity that leaves us indeed with a lugubrious holy, but defenseless and aghast before the joy of, for instance, a Baroque church. Such a church is luxuriant, joy-breathing, positively Mozartean in its vivacity—replete with rosy angels tumbling in unabashed enjoyment among impossibly fleecy clouds against an incredible blue heaven.

We shall not draw conclusions from that—only observe it and let it hang—that the gravity of a life determined by God, lived to the glory of God, is not necessarily incongruent with abounding joy. It is interesting to recall that the most rollicking music old periwig Bach ever wrote is not dedicated to the joy of tobacco (although he did that) or coffee (and he praised that) or the inventiveness among his fellow musicians, nor dedicated to the levity of the Count of Brandenburg, but *In Dir ist Freude* ("In Thee is Joy")!

The second statement is ascribed to Thomas Aquinas, surely not the playful or superficial type. Thomas did not affirm Christianity as a consolatory escape hatch, or an unguent to the scratchy personality, or a morale builder to a threatened republic—all contemporary malformations. But he did say, "It is of the heart of sin that people use what they ought to enjoy, and enjoy what they ought to use." Apart from the claim that it is *sin* that people do that, and apart from the seriousness of the situation if that statement should turn out to be true, is the statement reportorially so?

Yes, it is so, for all of us, and in many ways. Thomas is simply condensing here the profound dialectic of use and enjoyment that distorts and impoverishes life when it is not acknowledged and obeyed. To use a thing is to make it instrumental to a purpose, and some things are to be so used. To enjoy a thing is to permit it to be what it is prior to and apart from any instrumental assessment of it, and some things are to be so enjoyed.

I adduce a small example: it may bloom in our minds into bigger ones. Wine is to be *enjoyed;* it is not to be *used*. Wine is old in human history. It is a symbol of nature in her smiling beneficence—"close bosom friend of the maturing sun." That is why it has virtually everywhere and always been the accompaniment of celebrative occasions, the sign of gladness of heart. It is to be enjoyed; it is not to be used to evoke illusions of magnificence, or stiffen timidity with the fleeting certainty that one is indeed a sterling lad. Where it is enjoyed it adds grace to a truth; where it is used it induces and anesthetizes a lie.

Observe in Psalm 104 how the Old Testament psalmist who sought to glorify God and enjoy him forever stood in the midst of nature. God gives "wine to gladden the heart of man, oil to make his face shine." "This is the day which the Lord has made;" he exults, "let us rejoice and be glad in it." Why? Not primarily for what he can turn the day's hours into, but rather on the primal ground that there *are* days—unaccountable in their gift-character, just there. And here the psalmist is—permeable by all sensation:

[margin note: used vs. Enjoyed Examine: what is to be used & what is to be enjoyed]

texture, light, form, and movement, the cattle on a thousand hills. Thou sendest forth thy Spirit and they are! Let us rejoice and be glad in it!

> i thank You God for most this amazing
> day:for the leaping greenly spirits of trees
> and a blue true dream of sky;and for
>   everything
> which is natural which is infinite which is
>   yes[4]

we use our day vs. enjoy

It is of the heart of sin that humans use what they ought to enjoy.

It is also, says Thomas, of the heart of sin that humans are content to enjoy what they ought to use. Charity, for instance. Charity is the comprehensive term to designate how God regards humanity. That regard is to be used by humans for humans. That is why our Lord moves always in his speech from the source of joy, that humanity is loved by the holy, to the theater of joy, that humans must serve the need of the neighbor. "Lord, where did we behold thee?" "I was in prison, hungry, cold, naked"—you enjoyed a charity that God gives for use.

we should enjoy charity & use it

If the creation, including our fellow creatures, is impiously used apart from a gracious primeval joy in it the very richness of the creation becomes a judgment. This has a

cleansing and orderly meaning for everything in the world of nature, from the sewage
we dump into our streams to the cosmic
sewage we dump into the fallout.

Abuse is use without grace; it is always a
failure in the counterpoint of use and enjoyment. When things are not used in ways
determined by joy in the things themselves,
this violated potentiality of joy (timid as all
things holy, but relentless and blunt in its
reprisals) withdraws and leaves us, not perhaps with immediate positive damnations
but with something much worse—the wan,
ghastly, negative damnations of use without
joy, stuff without grace, a busy, fabricating
world with the shine gone off, personal relations for the nature of which we have
invented the eloquent term, *contacts*, starting without beholding, even fornication
without finding.

God is useful. But not if he is sought for
use. Ivan, in *The Brothers Karamazov,* saw
that, and Dostoevsky meant it as a witness to
the holy and joy-begetting God whom he
saw turned into an ecclesiastical club to
frighten impoverished peasants with, when
he had his character say, "I deny God for
God's sake!"

All of this has, I think, something to say
to us as teachers and students to whom this
university is ever freshly available for

enjoyment and use. For consider this: the basis of discovery is curiosity, and what is curiosity but the peculiar joy of the mind in its own given nature? Sheer curiosity, without immediate anticipation of ends and uses, has done most to envision new ends and fresh uses. But curiosity does this in virtue of a strange counterpoint of use and enjoyment. Bacon declared that "studies are for delight," the secular counterpart of "glorify God and enjoy him forever." The Creator who is the fountain of joy, and the creation which is the material of university study, are here brought together in an ultimate way. It is significant that the university, the institutional solidification of the fact that studies are for delight, is an idea and a creation of a culture that once affirmed that humans should glorify God and enjoy him forever.

Use is blessed when enjoyment is honored. Piety is deepest practicality, for it properly relates use and enjoyment. And a world sacramentally received in joy is a world sanely used. There is an economics of use only; it moves toward the destruction of both use and joy. And there is an economics of joy; it moves toward the intelligence of use and the enhancement of joy. That this vision involves a radical new understanding of the clean and fruitful earth is certainly so. But this vision, deeply religious in its genesis, is

not so very absurd now that natural damnation is in orbit, and humanity's befouling of
its ancient home has spread its death and dirt
among the stars.

5

The Treasure and the Vessel

NOTE: This sermon was preached to a special occasion: a conference of presidents and deans of church-related colleges who were inquiring about the definition and implementation of their responsibility toward church and learning.

Therefore, being engaged in this service by the mercy of God, we do not lose heart. We have renounced disgraceful, underhanded ways; we refuse to practice cunning or to tamper with God's word, but by the open statement of the truth we would commend ourselves to every man's conscience in the sight of God. And even if our gospel is veiled, it is veiled only to those who are perishing. In their case the god of this world has blinded the minds of the unbelievers, to keep them from seeing the light of the gospel of the glory of Christ, who is the likeness of God. For

*what we preach is not ourselves, but Jesus
Christ as Lord, with ourselves as your servants for Jesus' sake. For it is the God who
said, "Let light shine out of darkness," who
has shone in our hearts to give the light of
the knowledge of the glory of God in the face
of Christ.*

*But we have this treasure in earthen ves-
sels, to show that the transcendent power
belongs to God and not to us. We are afflicted
in every way, but not crushed; perplexed, but
not driven to despair; persecuted, but not forsaken; struck down, but not destroyed;
always carrying in the body the death of
Jesus, so that the life of Jesus may also be
manifested in our bodies.*

—2 Corinthians 4:1-10

Paul of Tarsus is a permanent embarrassment to all teachers of composition. There
are, to be sure, sections of his writing which
are tightly structured, integral, eloquently
wrought, and these are in the anthologies of
our Western literature. But the most of it is
not like that at all; and this part is as powerful as the architectonic and the rhetorical.

It almost seems as if the man couldn't keep
his mind on his work. What is actually the
case is that his passionate mind was so
absorbed by his work that the style is the
uncalculated reflection of the passion.

Buffon said that ". . . the style is the man himself," and few people in the realm of letters come through so loud and clear as Paul. The man had a big and a new and a revolutionary thing to say. He had, furthermore, to say it on the run. And not to a benign and well-conditioned religious culture, either; he had to speak in the angry and confusing criss-cross of organized and disorganized but pervasive powers that worked to distort and dilute his message or blunt the point of it by frantic attacks upon his person, his charter, his motives.

All of this was true of the Corinthian situation and true there with a vigor which served to heighten the very stylistic fact we are talking about.

This apprehension of the kind of person he was and this understanding of the kind of situation in which he had to do his declarative task make clear why it is simply impossible to preach from the Pauline Epistles by extracting from them a single text. For no matter where you start you find yourself in the situation of a small boy trying to eat taffy with his fingers and remain, betimes, presentable for the party! It's a bad job; it cannot really be done. Paul starts off on his development by stopping for a moment to beat off or beat down the crowding misapprehensions or burdensome distortions or literalistic reductions of what he is saying. And in the course of this rearguard action he finds it necessary to play over against his theme a counter-theme from the Old Testament. The very richness of his allusive and vehement mind conflates the two, so that the first theme builds up, now enriched and complicated by the contrapuntal structure. That is why the style is not episodic but fugal. And that is in part why a generation whose popular model of prose is the fatuous obviousness of *The Reader's Digest* has difficulties with the apostle to the Gentiles.

Our text is the seventh verse of the fourth chapter of the Second Epistle to the Corinthians. And we have only to look at the text to see that we cannot start with it, and to illustrate further what I have been saying about the impossibility of making a responsible sermon of a thread from a whole fabric. "But we have this treasure in earthen vessels . . ." the verse begins. Already we are in trouble. "But" indicates that something is about to be asserted over against a previously stated position. Paul's argument is characteristically sprinkled with this way of opening a paragraph. "Therefore," he says, or "Well, then . . ." or "So" or "Now if . . ." Such phrases are, as it were, a thumb back over the shoulder of the particular statement telling us that here is no epigram meant to shine in unreflected light or no statement extractable from a structured argument.

"But," he says. So let us follow the direction of the apostolic thumb and build in the background. Ideally we should go all the way back and begin with the opening of the letter and the first two chapters of it, for there we behold a tormented and an honest man making an almost pathetically loving apologia for misunderstood actions. His duties which have kept him away from Corinth have been interpreted as cowardice. And when he talks of the afflictions which have beset him he half knows that this recital will be understood as boasting. At the end of chapter two Paul pulls himself up, as it were, above this preliminary mire of suspicion that he has had to deal with and in a sentence of wonderful gallantry acknowledges that the glorious content of his word is too fermentingly alive for the fragility of the vessel, but affirms that he is nevertheless called to be a vessel and proposes to get on with the business! "For we are the aroma of Christ to God . . . a fragrance from life to life. Who is sufficient for these things? For we are not . . . peddlers of God's word; but as men of sincerity as commissioned by God, in the sight of God we speak in Christ."

Having thus cleared the decks, so to speak, Paul gets to the real problem which is the immediate context of our text, the immediate situation necessary for us here today if we are to understand his, "But we have this treasure . . ."

The problem is this: by what right does this little Jew dare to displace a massive tradition, subsume the noble old under a fiery new, pile up the evidence for the role of the ethnic religions in their venerable antiquity, their cultural creativity—and in the same of one Event, Christ, both fulfill them and sweep them all aside!

Bold and astonishing is the answer! "You!" he says, "you yourselves are our letters of recommendation, written on your hearts, to be known and read by all men." You are literally letters from Christ to the world, delivered by me, to be sure, but not written by me. For the Spirit of the living God is not only the content of the message, he is the writer of it; and the warm tablets of your hearts announce to the world that a strange possibility has become an empirical actuality—a congregation of people in this dying world who, in the process of their finitude, ". . . have passed from death to life."

Paul here is the complete pragmatist. People can be given this faith-relation to God whereby death is overcome because people have been given it, and here we are! Problems of epistemology there are, to be sure, and they are not improper or trivial, but if they become the primary and normative way to inquire into the fact of faith they repudiate what the message says about God: that he is alive, that his Spirit is not a static idea only to be investigated, that because he is God he accomplishes what he purposes.

And that is why, continues the apostle, we have the kind of confidence we have. Our confidence is not a sober assessment of our religious capacities or of our moral resoluteness, "not that we are sufficient of ourselves to claim anything as coming from us; our sufficiency is from God, who has qualified us to be ministers of a new covenant, not in a written code but in the Spirit; for the written code kills, but the Spirit gives life."

So we come to the opening of the chapter of our text. "Therefore, being engaged in this service by the mercy of God, we do not lose heart." May we not pause here for a moment and ponder whether that sentence might not be the banner to fly over this entire enterprise in the days ahead? "Therefore"! That says to us that in a profound sense we did not create the issue that brings us here; we are not the creators or stockholders of that in the world of humanity and culture which we propose here to discuss. "By the mercy of God," the text says. "I come to kindle a fire on the earth," says the Lord. And "I have been laid hold of," says the apostle—which is his word for our word vocation.

"Therefore, being engaged in this service . . ." "Service" has become a cheap word wherewith to set forth what is here said. The text reads, *Dia touto, echontes ten diakonian tauten*—and *diakonian* is but weakly rendered "service." We think of the service industries, the TV repairmen, and the dry cleaners. It's a thud to realize that *diakonian* in the New Testament means most centrally "worship," i.e., the entire responses of the entire man to the convulsing reality of God in the historical Christ. "Therefore, being engaged [that is, caught up] in this [worship] by the mercy of God, we do not lose heart!"

We don't lose heart for the single reason that the well we are pumping from is not the human, exhaustible, ambiguous, and vacillating well of our own hearts. We are not, in our terms, dependent upon the supply of our religious experience. Paul had a religious experience, to be sure. It made him an apostle, but it was not the content of his apostleship. It made his career; it was not the message of his career. It was the occasion of his being an ambassador; it was not the stuff in the portfolio. He got knocked off his horse by God, to be sure, but he never made a gospel out of the excitement of being knocked off a horse.

What then is the event from God before which Paul is broken into a new being, disorganized into a new organization, known into a new possibility of knowing, and loved into a new fullness of loving?

In order to declare this event the apostle is compelled to reach as far back as the primordial event of all existence to find an analogy huge enough to set it forth. Hear now how he sets it forth! "For what we preach is not ourselves, but Jesus Christ as Lord, with ourselves as your servants for Jesus' sake. For it is the God who said, 'Let light shine out of darkness,' who has shone in our hearts to give the light of the knowledge of the glory of God in the face of Christ."

Because that statement is the content of what Paul in the next sentence calls "this treasure," and because the having of this treasure in "earthen vessels" is the root problem of the vocation of the Christian college, it is necessary to be scientifically obedient to the religious particularity of the language Paul uses here. If this appears pedantic, recall that this sermon is not addressed to "the person on the street"; it is addressed rather to people who have in resolute purpose come in off the street with the announced intention of giving something beyond casual thought to a vexing problem.

"The light of the knowledge of the glory of God in the face of Christ." Three things in that statement must be responsibly attended to. First, what is the nature of this knowledge? When biblical speech puts light and knowledge together this way it intends to say that this knowledge is practical knowledge for the whole person to the end that that person's life shall be saved. It is not knowledge of nature, although interpretive of nature. It is not merely speculative knowledge, although it engenders and enriches speculation. It is not propositional truth, although it must seek to make affirmations having propositional integrity. It is a knowledge which has an absolute practicality because it illuminates humanity's central anxiety, lostness, and hurt; and because it heals what it reveals.

Second, what is the boundary of this knowledge? Observe that the apostle does not say, ". . . to give the light of the knowledge of God." He says rather, ". . . to give the light of the knowledge of the glory of God." The term glory is not here either a homiletical fillup or an unconscious piece of Semitic rhetoric. It is rather a deeply religious affirmation that God in his naked reality is not available to humanity. The term glory conveys a profound acknowledgement that the ultimate who dwells in light unapproachable is nevertheless the light that lighteth everyone that cometh into the world, and that this light unapproachable is nevertheless inescapable.

This glory is at once and always a lure, a burden, and a passion. It at once constitutes our personhood and relentlessly troubles our personhood with unextinguishable dreams. It is this glory which the heavens declare but do not deliver; it is this glory which, aflame between the cherubim and seraphim, crumples the young Isaiah with the antiphonal song, "Holy, Holy, Holy is the Lord of hosts; the whole earth is full of his glory." It is this glory to which Gerard Manley Hopkins points in his sonnet:

> The world is charged with the grandeur of
>   God.
> It will flame out, like shining from shook
>   foil;
>
> Because the Holy Ghost over the bent
> World broods with warm breast and will ah!
> Bright wings.[1]

Third, what is the content of this knowledge? "The light of the knowledge of the glory of God in the face of Christ." The face of Christ (*en prosopo Christou*) here does not mean merely the look of Jesus or the sweetness or magnanimity or bearing of Jesus. It means rather the entire action of God in a human being of earth who became obedient absolutely, so that in him alone we behold the absolute relation to the absolute, and in him alone we have the locus and face of what it means to be human.

So now we come to the summary statement which suggests how the three terms of our theme—Christian, Vocation, College—may be related. The treasure is given in the mercy of God in the gift of Christ. It is this treasure which is pointed to when we use the adjective Christian of our colleges; it is this treasure which troubles us when we ask the practical question of our obedience to our vocation. And that all comes out, in its promise and in its problems, when we confront the text, "But we have this treasure in earthen vessels."

In that word *but* is the entire problem of Christ and culture, the problem of the administration of the given treasure by the earthen vessels in which we have it, in which alone we can actualize it. This term *but* is the starting point of Christian theology—and its ultimate boundary.

There are, to be sure, two ways of getting around this built-in embarrassment. The first is to relax the meaning of the terms "treasure" and "vessel." Roman Catholic educational theory and practice is a possibility because the earthen character of the vessel is repudiated, and the glory of the treasure is postulated of the vessel. The authenticity of the treasure is extended to the declaration that the vessels which bear it forth are divinely accredited.

The other way around the embarrassment is so singlemindedly to adore the treasure as to ignore the fact that a vessel is for carrying, storing, pouring, making a thing available for use in the life of culture.

"But we have this treasure in earthen vessels." And we are here only because neither of these ways is open to us. And as we search for other ways let us be aware of the temptation to suppose that by taking thoughts we can devise a vessel—philosophical, ethical, cultic, or curricular—which shall transcend the earthen character of all vessels. Some vessels are better than others, and to fashion these each generation must be inventively obedient. But no vessel can accredit a treasure or guarantee its delivery.

That we do so ardently long for an accredited vessel and that this longing is a temptation, let us clarifyingly acknowledge. Oh, that we might find a verifying process, or a clear, unambiguous way, or an assured methodology wherewith to overcome the dialectic of an immeasurable treasure and the fragility but necessity of all vessels! With what envy do we all behold the steady refinement of methodologies in the sciences, physical and social, the ordered ways of philosophical enquiry, the tangibility of the research methods of the historian!

Perhaps the way of obedience is suggested to us if we hear Paul out to the end of the section. "But we have this treasure in earthen vessels, to show that the transcendent power belongs to God and not to us." How transparent that sentence is to all that pertains to the glory and the holiness of God! For through it we see God's entire way with humanity, a way that wins by losing, that redeems by dying, that lifts humans up by going down. And is all of this not continuous with the glory of God in the face of Christ as we behold him lifted up, not upon an assured throne but upon a cross, the very shape of a dialectical?

Relentlessly stretched between the treasure and the earthly vessel, may we not in our time and for our generation and in many faithful ways bear embarrassed witness that the transcendent power belongs indeed to God and not to us? The stretching belongs to the faithfulness. The treasure can never be packaged, for it is God himself. These vessels can never resign; he commands that they be, that they contain and convey, that they celebrate the treasure.

And as we come now to the end, hear how Paul does what he says, lives out in concrete career the stretched life between treasure and vessel. As we hear him speak of his own life in living words torn up by the roots from his own tormented and joyous existence, let us take heart! For why should we assume that because we come to this place in pullman or aircraft, we can be disciples at second hand! "We are afflicted in every way, but not crushed; perplexed, but not driven to despair; persecuted, but not forsaken; struck down, but not destroyed; always carrying in the body the death of Jesus, so that the life of Jesus may also be manifested in our bodies."

Grant us, O Lord, we beseech thee, to be faithful vessels of thy treasure. Give us the grace to know a treasure when we see it; the grace to be vessels when called; the discernment which keeps them from confusion and the obedience which keeps them together. Amen.

6

Epiphany, Glory, and 63rd Street

Arise, shine; for your light has come,
    and the glory of the LORD *has risen upon*
            you.
For behold, darkness shall cover the earth,
    and thick darkness the peoples;
but the LORD *will arise upon you,*
    and his glory will be seen upon you.
And nations shall come to your light,
    and kings to the brightness of your rising.

Lift up your eyes round about, and see;
    they all gather together, they come to
            you;
your sons shall come from far,
    and your daughters shall be carried in the
            arms.
Then you shall see and be radiant,
    your heart shall thrill and rejoice;
because the abundance of the sea shall be
            turned to you,

> *the wealth of the nations shall come to*
> *you.*
> *A multitude of camels shall cover you,*
> *the young camels of Midian and Ephah;*
> *all those from Sheba shall come.*
> *They shall bring gold and frankincense,*
> *and shall proclaim the praise of the*
> LORD.
>
> —*Isaiah 60:1-6*

We are still within the church season of the Epiphany of our Lord, and the sermon proposes some reflections upon the single word that dominates all the biblical passages, prayers, and hymns that the community has for hundreds of years remembered and used during this post-nativity period.

The word is the *glory*. But with this term, as with some others that carry heavy freight in a cult and a culture, one must walk around and have regard for a number of facts and notions if one is to avoid a too thin and single a meaning.

We begin that complication-in-order-to-clarification by reflecting upon what is intended by two affirmations that are often made in university pulpits. The first one is that the Christian confession of faith is other and more than the mind's acquiescence in propositions. That means to say that faith is a total act, that propositions have their specifying function, and that the fulfillment of this function does not add up to faith. The second affirmation is that humane studies should be cherished in a university; and that means to say that the humanities are the announcement and record of the depth and amplitude and variety of the wildly human story, and that attention to such studies discourages that over-simplification whose moral end and evil is idolatry.

The concern expressed in both of those affirmations is made specific when we ask after the meaning of the phrase *the glory*, and, in asking that, recall how the church uses language. When the church is not merely relating an episode, reporting, or exhorting, and when she is trying to point to promises and meanings in life she is always conducting what Mr. T. S. Eliot called a new ". . . raid on the inarticulate." She of course is not alone in this frantic business. All language in its most grave effort is an attempt to point to what it cannot clutch, to evoke the suspicion of magnitudes it cannot specify, to invite the mind to entertain the possibility that there are realities beyond the operational, and meanings that have no less force because their allure is more steady than precise.

It is indeed possible that we may, at this moment in culture, be more than usually cordial to this truth about language. The nature of things, the way things are in all realms of knowledge is being disclosed as more and more opaque at the same time that our operational use of things is more successful. This fact sets up a certain disturbance in the mind, and may in fact account for the reentrance into human speech of certain kinds of words which were, not so long ago, regarded as obstructive to thought.

The Oxford English Dictionary has one and a half columns about *glory;* and it is not until usage number 6 that it comes within gunshot of what might make sense in the first sentence of the lesson read from Isaiah, "Arise, shine; for your light has come, and the glory of the LORD has risen upon you." The obvious matters are cleared up first. Glory, we are told, means majesty, honor, pride, a state proper to accumulated accomplishments, and such like. We are informed that the term is vulgarly used as a "mere exclamation of delight in the worship of some religious sects." These are not specified, on the ground I suppose that Oxford some centuries ago made up its mind about which is the proper and not vulgar sect. But we are also informed, in a delightful and half-embarrassed aside, that certain low fellows of the baser sort have a household term, "glory-hole!" This is defined as "a box, drawer, receptacle in which things are heaped together without any order or tidiness."

Now that seems to advance us toward the set of mind we need! By the precision of the image—a precision that the vulgar so often and so shockingly achieve—we are led to know what we need to know about this word. Without order, all kinds of classification—defying stuff! Transcategorical, as it were!

Against such a cautionary background then, let us attend to the way the word glory works in the two Epiphany lessons read in our hearing a few moments ago. When Isaiah speaks of the rising glory of the Lord, he presupposes backward, and he images forward. Back of his statement, and loading it from Israel's fund of experience and richness of language was this: God is what is originating, creative, absolutely holy. He is the ground, the source of life, the core intention of all that is. And the glory is the signature of his form and presence. The glory is the light the holy gives off; it is the effulgence of that utter nucleus which is in and through all things but captured by none.

The glory partakes of the character of a secret. One's name is a symbol of the unimpartable and unique secret of the self: to tell the name is to disclose the self. Moses was at one and the same time told the *name* of the Lord, and admitted to see his glory.

Whenever and wherever in Israel's battle with her God she is forced to define her reality in that relationship the glory appears; in her recalcitrance she is smitten by it; in her quiet devotion it is the term for the health and glow of rightness with God; in her exile and despair it is the glory, departed but unforgettably luring, that shapes her heartbreaking songs by the rivers of Babylon; and when she is home again in heart and foot and worship it is at Mount Zion, "The place where the glory dwells." All of that is back of the cry of the prophet to a people sunk in apathy, prostrate in despair: "Arise, shine; for your light has come, and the glory of the Lord is risen upon you."

But forward, too, the prophet images forth the glory, and thick material images are drawn dripping like a sponge from the Eastern place. Sight, sound, smell, the barbaric color and movement of common life become the bearers of the promise that all things, though not yet seen, are in motion toward a restoration. Jerusalem stands there on her high ridge: to the East across the wadis are the further flat sands. "A multitude of camels shall cover you, the young camels of Midian and Ephah." And to the West, where falling from the escarpment the land slopes away to the sea—the vision sees the crowding white sails—"all those from Sheba shall come.

They shall bring gold and frankincense, and shall proclaim the praise of the LORD."

What's really going on here? Back of and informing the flaming incandescence of these images, what is being affirmed about God and humanity? Except we suspect that the confluence of images can be as maieutic to faith as a procession of propositions we shall neither hear nor understand. It is here affirmed that there is in nature and history a holy possibility for the fulfillment of all things; that that possibility is, and is Holy, because all things exist in the ultimate placenta which is God the creator and sustainer. And the comprehensive term for that perception and that faith is the glory.

Christian worship has always understood this. If one seeks for a word common to the entire spectrum of corporate acknowledgment and adoration, and considers all in that enormous range from calculated Gregorian intervals to the spontaneous outbursts of Appalachian shout and song, from the unearthly shimmer of Palestrina to the rocking rhythms of Negro song—it is the force of the glory that is attested.

The image has a rich and steady career in Israel and church; it inwardly controls every episode, and shines like a light beckoning to ever fresh interpretation of every statement. Just as "the heavens declare the glory of

God"—for they are a transparency symbolic of the ineffable glory "which thou hast set above the heavens"—so therefore Israel dared not name the glory in a proper noun. But this glory, uncapturable in category and concept, is nevertheless that which formed and forms this people Israel to the mad faith that neither nature nor history has slipped nor been snatched from holy hands.

Only thus can the full symbolic measure of the meaning of the Christian identification of the Christ and the glory be suspected. When, in the nativity stories, "the glory of the Lord shone round about," and when the child was greeted as the "glory of thy people Israel," the background is given for the claim that in Christ the glory has concretely come fleshly nigh—"and we beheld his glory, full of grace and truth." And when the darkness of death failed to smother a life luminous with the glory, and the community affirmed him to be alive and creative of nothing less than a new being for men, they put it this way: "Christ was raised from the dead by the *glory* of the Father"!

So too in one of the summary paragraphs in the New Testament that has the sonority of celebration as well as the gravity of a huge faith, it is affirmed that this glory is the life of and irradiates all that is. Four times in the first chapter of Ephesians we are told that the

apex of life is to *be* "to the praise of his
glory." The glory is the reality that fills the
space that ontological inquiries mark out; it
is the ultimate ambience in which the mys-
tery of our restless lives swing to and fro; it
is the persisting allure that draws and drives
all things beyond the vain glory of penultimate meanings. It sings in nerve and blood
in D. H. Lawrence, in the arching specula-
tions of Plotinus, and it meets us as a gift, an
evocation, and a demand in every dirty
street, every hurt upturned face, every failure
of fulfillment on the streets of this world.

Very quickly, then, these three: *gift, evocation, demand.*

I. It is a gift
Everyone who has ever got stuck in the stick-
iness of the *possible* as it meets one in the
ever-so-hopeless stasis of the *actual* knows
this joyful burden to be a gift! One suddenly,
or gradually, has come to *see;* and this creative fusion and vision and form and emerg-
ing patterns one knows with immediate and
never-diminishing certainly to have been
given. There are, to be sure, requirements
given with the seeing; and to these one must
attend in prosaic labor, thought, experiment,
and discipline; but one's exercise of these
corollary activities never adds up to a kind of
justification or deserving. Every vision of

fullness and authenticity and justice and of a possible goodness in life has this unextinguishable gift-character.

II. It is an evocation

The vision of the glory, the rising light of the holy that is "the light that lighteth every man that cometh into the world . . ." is God's way of getting heavenly song upon earthly streets, the ecstasy of the cherubim into plain deeds of justice among the creatures.

The hard-nosed of this world may feel all of this to be nonsense, and see no connection between prayer, praise, and men and women caring for fellow creatures in the glory. But a lifetime of caring is a hard-nosed fact too; and when Saint Francis dealt with a leper in Christ's name, he was not necessarily deluded.

All of this is caught in a few lines of verse by Gerard Manley Hopkins. This is manifestly close-stuff, and not for the street; but we are, after all, for this hour, in off the street, and this is an arrogantly close university!

> As kingfishers catch fire, dragonflies draw
>   flame;
> As tumbled over rim in roundy wells
> Stones ring; like each tucked string tells,
>   each hung bell's

Bow swung finds tongue to fling out broad
    its name;
Each mortal thing does one thing and the
    same:
Deals out that being indoors each one
    dwells;
Selves—goes itself; *myself* it speaks and
    spells,
Crying *What I do is me: for that I came.*
I say more: the just man justices;
Keep grace: that keeps all his goings graces;
Acts in God's eye what in God's eye he is—
Christ—for Christ plays in ten thousand
    places,
Lovely in limbs, and lovely in eyes not his
To the Father through the features of men's
    faces.[1]

III. The glory is demand

"That we should be to the praise of his glory"
sounds like an impossibly abstract hook to
hang the conduct of life upon. Everything is
against it; everything, that is, except fact,
experience, and the interior dynamics of
human history. A paragraph from Gilbert
Chesterton puts the matter better than I can.

The 18th century theories of the social con-
tract were demonstrably right insofar as
they meant that there is at the back of all

historic government an idea of content and cooperation. But they really were wrong insofar as they suggested that men had ever aimed at order or ethics directly by a conscious exchange or interests. Morality did not begin by one man saying to another, "I will not hit you if you will not hit me"; there is no trace of such a transaction. There is a trace of both men having said "We must not hit each other in the holy place." They gained their morality by guarding their religion. They did not cultivate courage. They fought for the shrine, and found they had become courageous. They purified themselves for the altar, and found that they were clean. The Ten Commandments which have been found substantially common to mankind were merely military commands; a code of regimental orders, issued to protect a certain Ark across a certain desert. Anarchy was evil because it endangered the holy. And only when they made a holy day for God did they find they had made a holiday for men.[2]

Amen.

7

Acceptance, Human and Divine

We then that are strong ought to bear the infirmities of the weak, and not to please ourselves. Let every one of us please his neighbor for his good to edification. For even Christ pleased not himself; but, as it is written, The reproaches of them that reproached thee fell on me. For whatsoever things were written aforetime were written for our learning, that we through patience and comfort of the scriptures might have hope. Now the God of patience and consolation grant you to be likeminded one toward another according to Christ Jesus: that ye may with one mind and one mouth glorify God, even the Father of our Lord Jesus Christ.

Wherefore receive ye one another, as Christ also received us to the glory of God. Now I say that Jesus Christ was a minister of the circumcision for the truth of God, to confirm the promises made unto the fathers:

*and that the Gentiles might glorify God for
his mercy.*

—Romans 15:1-9

It is widely assumed that, while certain
admonitions in the gospel of God are profound and useful in the sphere of personal
relations, their content can be abstracted
from the structure of that gospel and forth-
with applied. There is a sense in which that is
true and another sense in which it is not true.
It is true in the sense that the self requires
love, given and received, for its own preser-
vation. And therefore the words of our Lord
about love confirm the blunt aphorism of a
contemporary study—"Love or Perish."

But the assumption that this counsel to
love can release its usefulness if abstracted
from the entire structure of the gospel of
God is not true in the sense that the love
which the gospel speaks about is not a sort
of free resource, loosely floating about in
interpersonal spaces, which has only to be
caught, condensed, and utilized to do its
health-giving work.

The Gospels never speak about love like
that. Love is always an aspect of, or a function
of, or the designate of a response to something
said about *God:* God's people, God's house,
God's law, God's historically manifested care—
"I have loved the habitations of thy house"; "O

how I love thy law." Supremely in the Old Testament, it comes out in such a statement as "Thou shalt love the Lord thy God with all thy heart, and mind, and strength"—and, *therefore*, "thy neighbor as thyself." Supremely in the New Testament, in the statement "Herein is love, not that we love God, but that he loved us."

It is necessary to get this matter of redemptive love's availability for life very straight, and on two grounds. First, the structure of the word of God, which is that humans are beloved of God and that with a huge, deep, undeviating relentlessness. This structure has an integrity, an inner logic. It is the truth. But not a truth which can be pushed around, manipulated, used for purposes purely analgesic, cosmetic, or lubricative in the field of human relations. It is a truth that must be received and appropriated within the structure of the whole truth.

And, second, this truth is bitterly needed. For the gospel never affirms that love as a general human resource floating about as an available potency waiting only to be grasped—the gospel never claims *that* to be redemptive. But we *do* claim it; and the affable magazines with modern kitchens or pretty dresses on the cover are its unholy scriptures. What is bitter about our need for the truth is simply that if we fall for an untruth about love we are built up for a let-down. If men and women, for instance, are encouraged to believe that in the hot furnace of loving personal relations ultimate redemption can be found, several bitter things occur: they write too large checks on one another; they frantically turn to love to deliver a redemption which love itself was never intended to supply; they eat one another up instead of building one another up. The entire weight of personal life is on a single hook, and when the hook pulls out, they are bitter. All exposed idolatry engenders bitterness, and this is an idolatry.

Let us now inquire into the place and power and function of love as it is revealed in the drama of God's love for humanity as that drama is implied and pointed to in a single verse in the letter to the Romans. We shall get at it in this way—first, analyze what is signified by the popularity of a current term in the personality sciences; second, place over against this term a characteristic term in personal relations used in the New Testament; third, point out what the difference means.

First, then, the term. A bright new word is on the loose—or, better, an old word with an assumed bright new potential. The term *acceptance* has become a capital term in psychological discourse. It embodies a frantic residual possibility for human relations, now that other relations are so faulty. The term *acceptance* is an operational center for an increasing volume of verse, short stories, and TV shows. It lubricates bull-sessions to the degree that we wonder how we ever got along without it. It is well on the way to designating a personal philosophy, a social habit, a psychological stance, a cosmic analgesic—virtually a total theology. Let us call the roll of its content: *acceptance* is the embodiment of a philosophy. Nothing for sure can be known; nothing is more certain than other things; no way is better than other ways; no structure of vision, quest, discipline, or evaluation is higher than others. No person is closer than another to the reality of authentic personhood, for all live in pathos, deception, and pitiable pride.

And therefore *acceptance* becomes also the term for an attitude proper to this philosophy. Where nothing means anything there is a common democracy in nothing. Where there are no requirements there can be no judgments. Where there are no judgments there is no gravity and there are no issues. And, therefore, the only mature stance in the world and among humans is acceptance.

From this rich ground the term goes on to gather even more around itself. It is a philosophy appropriate to the manifest impossibility of having a philosophy. It is an attitude appropriate to the absurdity of anything so grave as an attitude. Out of this passionless passion, this negation with reversed English, is generated a gospel. The terms of this gospel, to be sure, are wan, but they have a certain gallantry. "The world," as Dietrich Bonhoeffer says, "has come of age." We know what we know, we have seen what we have seen. And we do not propose to be taken in. We may be a beaten generation; but we will be damned if we will be seduced by febrile enthusiasms or unstructured affirmations. "You cannot fool us," as one of our own poets has said, "by the redness of little leaves opening stickily. They are all gone—the beautiful, the proud, and the brave—and I do not consent." And therefore acceptance is the only available alternative that makes any sense.

This is a posture that at least is not banal or indecent before the truth—that the meaning of history is that history has no meaning. If we indeed "look back in anger," then let us have the candor to look *out* with acceptance. The quiet acquiescence in acceptance is more integral than the noisy protestations of people who think they have been cheated. For to protest that one has been cheated presupposes a human inheritance of meaning and worth. Now that the presupposition is no longer viable the anger and hurt are obviously infantile.

Acceptance, therefore, is what one might call the necessary ethics of nihilism and despair. It is the name for that right relationship of each of us to the other, a tolerable prescription for getting on, now that we, knowing there is no place to go, do not propose to be unseemly in our eagerness to get there. This gospel is the inaudible gospel of millions who never think about it, and it has developed around itself a sort of liturgy of nihilism. We have an entire vocabulary that operates within this liturgy. People call each other "darling" and turn on bright smiles of terrible fragility. The sacramental cup of the whole dance of death is the martini—dry, sunless, thin, and sharp. And here too, as in the history of all arts, earlier impure forms are refined toward completeness, so that in the more advanced circles of acceptance the humane olive has been replaced by the caustic onion, and the gibson emerges. The cult of acceptance is polite. Polite as hell. It has its own grace: the graciousness of no expectation, the suavity of emptiness, the courtesy of non-significance.

There are dimensions to our way of acceptance, however, which trouble us. For if I accept a person, identifying their wholeness with the sheer phenomenology of their existence, I have by that acceptance agreed to evacuate them of their freedom. I have agreed with them that the self they present to me is all there is and, in a sense, have confirmed them in the cynical, monodimensional pathos of their plight. Meaning to show that there is value in them and in me—at least this residual value of our mutual acceptance—I have actually announced to them that, having no barriers to acceptance, no judgmental attitudes, there is nothing valuable, either for me or for them.

And now what shall be said to all of this? I propose to say something, but it is necessary to be quite clear in what role I presume to say it. What I want to say I say in my office as a minister of the gospel. I could not possibly say it from any other position or on any other ground. I stand where everyone stands. I know no way out for myself beyond ways out that are available to everybody. But in my role as a listener to the gospel, a witness to what is said there to all of us—in that role I am alone important in this place and at this moment.

A "listener," a "witness," an "ambassador"—these are the New Testament terms used for the function which I exercise now. The witness is to behold and then bear witness to something which has occurred within experience but which was in no sense a product of it. The

task is to set over against the story of humanity the concrete, lived-out story of God as
that story has been made concrete in an
actual human person. This person did not die
in bed, tranquilly dispensing religious truths
to devoted followers, but was beaten and died
an awesome death. Nor is it the task of the
ministry to guarantee that people should
believe this story (remember the statements in
the Gospels: "flesh and blood hath not
revealed it unto thee, but my Father which is
in heaven"); it is the task of the ministry to
tell the story. We conclude, therefore, this
morning by setting over against the beat
gospel of acceptance a particular facet of the
larger gospel of God.

From the fifteenth chapter of Romans, hear
this verse: "Wherefore receive ye one another,
as Christ also received us to the glory of God."
This verse declares that God has spoken. The
word is not silent. Christ is what God has said.
All of this speaking is for our learning, in
order that we might have hope. This is the
context of the verse we have read. This is to
say that every person's structure of possibility
is here ensconced in nothing less than God's
enormous deed of actuality in Jesus Christ. In
this deed is given to every person a new structure and a new dynamics of fellowship. The
whole difference between acceptance and
what the gospel says about human relations is

in the understanding of the word in the text which is translated "receive" in our English text. The Greek word is *proslambanesthe*, and the difference is as follows: acceptance is determination without presupposition. Reception is obedience in valuation because God has supremely evaluated. Acceptance is *my* action, limited in meaning to *my* meaning or *my* meaninglessness. To receive is obedience to God's action, limitless in both evaluation and potential, because both I and the received are standing under an immeasurable grace.

There is a story in the Old Testament which makes this point with wonderful eloquence. You recall the incident when the brothers of Joseph come back to him in Egypt, after Joseph, their once slave-sold brother, had achieved an important position in the empire. As Joseph reveals to them who he is they fall on their faces in embarrassment and fright, crying out to know whether Joseph will forgive them. Regard the wonderful depth of the reply which Joseph makes: "Forgive you? Do you think I am God?" Joseph knows, that is to say, that forgiving or not forgiving is *not his business at all!* As one who has been forgiven, he no longer has this election.

To receive a person in Jesus Christ because I have been received moves the entire action away from the realm of evaluation and its implied judgment. For value has no place in the realm of grace. Christianly speaking, I have value because God receives me; God does not receive me because I have value. A strangely other source of worthiness determines the action of God in Christ: neither the community which says of a Roman officer in a Jewish town, "He is worthy that you should do this thing"; nor the centurion's own evaluation, "I am not worthy." The evaluation of the holy endows both the outer-directed and the inner-directed valuations with a quite strange value—"and Jesus started down the road to the man's house."

All of this makes clear that a Christian doctrine of value must begin with a christly traffic upon our common history's road, not with history's own assessment of better or worse, acceptability or non-acceptability.

Advent, that is to say, is the theological, as well as the chronological, prolegomenon to Lent. The movement of the holy disrupts, confuses, and reestablishes on an utterly new ground every assessment and potentiality.

This is the mighty theological acceptance which alone can ground, save from cynicism and despair, all the strange receptions of earth.

8

Knowledge and Liberation

NOTE: This is an academical Christian address and was prepared for two occasions: an Honors Day convocation in a Roman Catholic college, and a commencement in a Lutheran college. It is some kind of commentary upon the identity of the central substance of our common Christian tradition that the same speech could be made in both situations.

You will know the truth, and the truth will make you free.

—John 8:32

I propose for our reflection on this occasion a text from Holy Scripture. The text is proper for today for it bears upon the life of the mind and presupposes its native appetite for truth, and it is relevant to the steady effort of this school to inquire how it ought order its life so as to honor and serve the truth.

"You will know the truth, and the truth will make you free."

Will you join me to consider that statement on two levels. The first level is simply as an epigram, a kind of general wise saying, a naked proposition having nothing to do with church, faith, or even with Jesus Christ who said it. So regarded—which is admittedly not a sufficient way to regard the statement—what might it mean?

A relation is postulated between truth and freedom. This relation is functional: truth is affirmed to be a force that liberates. Liberal education exists to try that out. Your years in this place and your response to its duties have been an experimental interview with that assumption.

When general collegiate occasions are used for exhortation they commonly fail of lasting effect and they are likely to be dull. I choose, therefore, rather to ask you to recall the claim of our proposition—that truth is a force that liberates—and suggest to you several actual liberations that truth so operating may accomplish in and for each of us. And you will excuse me if in an effort to make these descriptions specific and alive I speak of how these liberations have happened in my own life. As an academic person I have little hesitancy to do this on the ground that I have listened to a melancholy number of commencement speeches which, while rich in generality and heavy with counsel, lacked any evidence that the speaker was having or ever had any fun with the intellectual liberation he was praising!

I. The Truth liberates from the tyranny of loneliness

The mind has a native imperial largeness and it suffers from constriction. The individual exists at a particular intersection of the generally human in time and space, but has a dreaming capacity for other times and places and longs to go out to enfold them. And a person, regardless of the excitements of his or her particular time and space, is deeply lonely when such scope and traffic is either absent or not allowed. Studies called the humanities are so designated because they show us that way, open it, people it, and speed us on our way towards the heart's charter of fullness.

How does one get started on that way?— and by what employments do the steps of it gain firmness and speed and joy as we go along it?

When still an apple-munching urchin, I lived in a home that had many good books, but few of those pot-boiled series of boys' books whose literary level causes teachers of literature to blanch. But up the street there was a spoiled only child of a wealthy man whose room was literally lined with the gallant junk that boys love! I read straight around the room: the Rover Boys, the Motor Boys, and on to a stack of historical novels by a prolific author named A. J. Henry. That this stuff was inexact, even bad, history I now know. But it was full of incredible swordsmen and evil villains, gallant kings and lovely queens, barons and knights barging around gloomy crenellated castles at their dubious business.

What happened to a boy thus engaged? The world of privacy was invaded, the chance intersection of a single life was exploded out and back, the place of the alone was peopled, my time was placed in longer time and my place was given a context in many places.

It was but a short yet crucial jump from Henry to Sir Walter Scott—*Ivanhoe, Kenilworth, Quentin Durward*. So when, as a college sophomore in 1925, I came across Henry Adams' *Mont-Saint-Michel and Chartres*, the exciting bad gave me entrance to exciting good, the inexact third-rate had done such humanizing work as to sensitize for the first-rate. So it was that when eleven years later I went to Chartres I had so passed from junk to excellence that I entered that church not only as an adult theologically prepared to know and feel the power of Christ and the Virgin, but with my boyhood's horse tied outside and my boyhood's armour clanking on the ancient pavement!

II. Learning liberates from the tyranny of egocentricity

By egocentricity I mean a life understood and felt dominantly from the hot center of the tyrannical, demanding and stifling *self*. Learning disorganizes and complicates the stifling simplicity of the purely personal; it floods the self with a company of vital selves; it multiplies perspectives. One becomes for a season paranoid Ahab, stands in rigid pride with him on the bitter deck of the *Pequod* and talks back to all the great malignant whales of man's existence; one skulks among the furtive shadows of Notre Dame with Francois Villon and learns from him and with him the pathos of passingness and the mutability of all that is earthly lovely. One grows in sheer human astonishment before the soul's vast imaginative powers as one shares the world of the sisters Bronte who, with the Yorkshire moors for one world, people it with another. If one really responds to old Shakespeare's invitation, "For God's sake let us sit upon the ground and tell sad stories of the death of kings," one is matured toward a comprehension of the tragic boundedness of all mortality and given a sense for the reality of evil more demonically majestic than the episodes of his or her own life might supply. So one comes to know that Conrad's Kurtz, returning broken down the great brown river muttering only "the horror" is every person's life, and the horror is the relentless underside of every betrayed vision. And Dostoevsky's Ivan—how he wrestles with me and for me in my frequent rebellion before God, and by expanding my solitary trouble to the dimensions of a big and ancient problem puts me in my human place and makes me, if not at peace, no longer alone or egocentric in my dispeace.

How this release from egocentricity works in a person is caught in a quatrain from a poem "On Wenlock Edge," by Alfred Edward Housman. An English farmer, standing below the escarpment that bounds the valley of the Severn, is watching a storm so violent that it "bends the saplings double." Through the wind and the rain he can see crumbling ruins of old dwellings that had been erected during the Roman occupation of Britain seventeen centuries earlier. And he reflects,

Then, 'twas before my time, the Roman
At yonder heaving hill would stare,

The blood that warms an English yeoman,
The thoughts that hurt him, they were
    there.[1]

Related to this liberating power of shared experience is an essay recently published by my colleague, Professor Nathan Scott, Jr. Mr. Scott writes as follows:

> For surely . . . one of the great reasons for any adult consenting to devote a large measure of time to reading of novels (or any of the other forms of mimetic literature) is its insatiable craving for large images of human engagement in the life of the world, and images that have the power of increasing its own capacity to live. . . . We are most deeply drawn not to the artist whose personages are merely elements of his own personality but, rather, to him whose characters are a part of Nature and who therefore "make us feel that there is a world elsewhere"—that is, the world of which we are living members—and show something of how the human spirit goes about surviving in that world.[2]

And now to the second, incomparably more important, and specifically Christian meaning of the statement, "You will know the truth, and the truth will make you free."

The flat and unmodified affirmation that God's truth is available, invasive, and adequate in Christ, and that this truth bestows absolute freedom is a statement which differs in kind from all we have been saying.

Jesus was not here speaking of the furnishing and refinement of the mind in its engagement with other minds, or of the multifications of one's selfhood that sharing bestows, or of the intensification and enlargement of experience through vicarious participation in the life of our kind. For while it is true that human truth liberates us from loneliness and from egocentricity, such liberations, good and demonstrable as they are, are not a sufficient liberation. We are always tempted to believe that if small knowledge grants small liberations, enlargements of knowledge work larger liberations, and up the quantitive scale, as it were, until one achieves sufficient knowledge to secure an absolute liberation. But the interior drama of the mind in its knowing does not confirm that blithe logic, for all knowledge complicates as it expands; it generates ambiguity as it multiplies; its clarity is illuminative of ever deeper and intractable imprisonments. "He that increases knowledge increases sorrow" is indeed the testimony of humane wisdom.

O the mind, mind has mountains; cliffs of
     fall
Frightful, sheer, no-man-fathomed. Hold
     them cheap
Many who ne'er hung there. Nor does long
     our small
Durance deal with that steep or deep. Here!
     creep,
Wretch, under a comfort serves in a
     whirlwind: all
Life death does end and each day dies with
     sleep.[3]

The core of humanity's unfreedom is its self-imprisonment. Humans are slaves because they permit themselves to be enslaved to their self's tyrannical power. When Luther declared that "Man seeks himself in everything, even in God," he observed the core-fact of all human life. And in this observation he really understood the tragic context and demand of our Lord's saying, "If any man would come after me, let him deny himself . . ."

In the history of human reflection there is no more penetrating analysis of the interior dynamics of domination by the tyranny of the self, nor a profounder prolegomenon to the specific *place* of grace in the intellectual life than in the meditations of St. Augustine.

He affirms that human knowledge is determined by human love. We do not know truly because we do not love properly or amply. Right knowledge is a function of right love. And what is the actual history of humanity's love? Simply that we love ourselves—passionately, toughly, fiercely, relentlessly. This passion is the human pathos, and there is no adequate liberation, no salvation so long as its way and power be not broken and changed.

Unless and until the love with which I love finds its proper object in the love with which I am loved by God I am a prisoner of a love too small for love's heavenly nature and scope. The gospel declares that this human fact has been met by a sufficient godly act. Its name is Jesus Christ ". . . who loved us and gave himself for us."

And now, therefore, we are prepared to comprehend a deep, deep meaning of our text: the truth makes us free from the illusion that *truth as knowledge* is redemptive! In this liberation-by-personal-act the quasi-liberations of knowledge are disclosed and judged and overcome.

This understanding of the interior dynamics of God and love and knowledge and freedom is the *raison d'etre* of the church's steady effort in the world of education. Education is not redemptive because damnation is not simply ignorance or inaccuracy about fact. But knowledge is related to redemption because and insofar as it serves the truth, and the highest truth it proposes is that truth-as-knowledge is not redemptive. In that proposal we do not learn what is redemptive; we may, however, be liberated from the tyranny and the bitter falseness of redemptive claims that have no power to redeem. We may come to know the truth that makes us free from the vain hope in "truths" that do not add up to freedom. We may come, perhaps, to the place of Augustine and acknowledge with him: "Thou has formed us for thyself, O Lord, and our hearts are restless till they rest in thee."

Notes

Chapter 2

1. *Divine Comedy,* Paradiso, Canto XXXIII, trans., Cary.

2. A. C. Swinburne, "Hymn to Proserpine."

Chapter 4

1. This sermon was included in Franklin H. Littell, ed., *Sermons to Intellectuals* (New York: Macmillan, 1963).

2. "Advice to a Prophet" from *Advice to a Prophet and Other Poems,* copyright © 1959 and renewed 1987 by Richard Wilbur.

3. Isaiah 6:1-3.

4. E. E. Cummings, from "I thank You God for most this amazing". Copyright 1950, © 1978, 1991 by the Trustees from the E. E. Cummings Trust. Copyright © 1979 by George James Firmage, from *Complete Poems: 1904-1962* by E. E. Cummings, edited by George J. Firmage. Used by permission of Liveright Publishing Corporation.

Chapter 5

1. "God's Grandeur" in *Selected Poems and Prose* (Baltimore: Penguin, 1953), 27.

Chapter 6

1. An untitled poem in Gerard Manley Hopkins, *Selected Poems and Prose* (Baltimore: Penguin, 1953), 51.

2. *Orthodoxy* (London: Bodly Head Ltd., 1957), 107. Para. from *Orthodoxy* by G. K. Chesterton, © 1957. Used by permission of A P Watt Ltd. on behalf of The Royal Literary Fund.

Chapter 8

1. "On Wenlock Edge" from '*The Shropshire Lad*', *Collected Poems* (Alden Press, 1939) and *The Collected Poems of A. E. Housman*. Copyright 1965 by Henry Holt and Company, © 1967, 1968 by Robert E. Symons. Reprinted by arrangement with Henry Holt and Company, LLC. and The Society of Authors as the Literary Representative of the Estate of A. E. Housman.

2. "Society and the Self in Recent American Literature," *Union Seminary Quarterly Review* 18, no. 4 (May 1963).

3. An untitled poem in Gerard Manley Hopkins, *Selected Poems and Prose* (Baltimore: Penguin, 1953), 61.